Mark Rothko, *Saffron*. Painted 1957 (formerly Collection
Carlo Cardazzo). Rothko was exhibited at Biennale, 1958.

THE VENICE BIENNALE 1895-1968

from salon to goldfish bowl

THE VENICE BIENNALE 1895-1968

from salon to goldfish bowl

BY LAWRENCE ALLOWAY

NEW YORK GRAPHIC SOCIETY LTD.
Greenwich, Connecticut

Library of Congress
Catalog Card Number 68–13051
© Lawrence Alloway 1968
All rights reserved.
No part of this book may be
reproduced without
the permission of the publisher.
Printed and bound in
the United States of America.
Design by Wladislaw Finne.

for
sylvia,
in
venice

ACKNOWLEDGMENTS

I am grateful to Herbert Schutz, whose idea it was; to Umbro Apollonio, Curator of the Archivio Storico d'Arte Contemporanea della Biennale, who shared his knowledge with me; and to Sergio Pozzati, librarian of the Archivio, for his resourceful and untiring help. I want to thank Gloria Hodsoll for her translations in Venice and Simona Tuten and Marielù Marini for translations in New York. In addition, Dr. Tuten kindly assisted my research in many ways. Grace Glueck, Donelson F. Hoopes, Leo Castelli, and Maurice Tuchman promptly answered my questions, and Mary Joan Hall, librarian of the Solomon R. Guggenheim Museum, aided my last-minute checking. Jane Umanoff helped me to prepare the manuscript. Photographs are reproduced with permission of the Archivio, which supplied all but two; these (figs. 58 and 40) came from the Trustees of the Chatsworth Settlement, and the Leo Castelli Gallery.

CONTENTS

1   The Biennale in 1968   12
    The Biennale and Other Exhibitions   13
    The Biennale as a Structure   15
    The Pavilions   17
    Organization and Influence   18
    The Future of the Biennale   22
    The Biennale as a Party   23
    The Biennale as a Target   24

2   The Biennale as Super-Salon 1895-1914   30

    Illustrations: Historical Photographs   56

3   The Instability of Taste   82

4   The Biennale and Fascism 1920-42   92

5   Art and the Expanding Audience   120

6   The Avant-Garde in a Goldfish Bowl 1948-68   132

    Illustrations: Prize Winners   156

    List of Illustrations   182

    Bibliography   190

    Appendix: some statistics   192

    Index   194

THE
VENICE
BIENNALE
1895-1968
from salon to goldfish bowl

ONE

THE BIENNALE
IN 1968

The Biennale and Other Exhibitions

In 1968, in addition to the Biennale in Venice, there were one hundred and twelve other official exhibitions and fairs in Italy, some international, some local. The subjects ranged from an International Aeronautical Show in Venice to an International Container Convention in Genoa, from automation in Milan to children's books in Bologna.[1] The contents of the Biennale are works of art, and for this reason, we tend to reserve them from participation in this orgy of contact and communication. We tend to relate them to humanism rather than to the competitive area of fairs and shows. For reasons that will emerge later, our preference has been for works of art as symbols of permanence rather than as complex structures subject to numerous interpretations. However, art is physically and conceptually mobile, which means that it can be seen in various contexts. As it is subject to the communications network of our time, physically or in terms of reproductive processes, some of art's talismanic solidity is reduced by the increase in connectivity. A work that was executed for a chapel, and stays there, can be connected with fewer art works and environments than a work that is movable. Even here, the imaginary museum of photographs makes possible the re-contextualizing of the most sacred and monumental art. The Venice Biennale is not only a demonstration of art's contextual shifts; it is, during a period of unprecedented exhibition-activity, the major institution.

The 1966 Biennale showed 2,785 works by artists from thirty-seven countries; attendance was 181,383, with eight hundred art critics, journalists, and free-wheelers in addition. Sales amounted to around 141,684,690 lire. These figures indicate the magnitude of the exhibition. It is large enough to bring into the foreground our ideas about the artist and his audience, the relation of the individual to the new scale and speed of international communications. Those who gravitate to an elitist view of art regard the Biennale's abundance as a dilution of art's neat essence. On the other hand, left-wing critics oppose the show too, because of the preponderance of international styles without manifest social usefulness.

What I propose here is an outline of the Biennale as an organization, one that in its history touches on unsettled problems of art in society. There are many studies of artists, schools of art, media, and iconography, but not much has been written on the distribution of art. The groups that artists formed in the past to organize their own profession have been thoroughly investigated,[2] but their more recent means of contact with an increasingly large public have been less discussed. The tendency is to study the work of art as an object, rather than as part of a communication system. As an entity in time the Biennale has been adaptive to social and political change; it has changed basically, at least three times, but it has not lost its core identity, its legibility as an institution.

In addition to the solid shows, such as the Venice Biennale, there are some that, though large, only simulate the reality of the others. It is important to clarify the comparative value of such exhibitions. Consider the Salon International de Galeries-pilotes, held at the Musée Cantonal des Beaux-Arts, Lausanne. A pilot gallery is defined as one that is devoted to the discovery of talent rather than to its merchandising, or one not identified with a constant esthetic position. Betty Parsons in New York is an example of the former and Denise René in Paris of the latter. At Lausanne all expenses are carried by the participating galleries, and indeed, they install their own sections. Under the circumstances it would need rigorous control if the exhibition were to be more than simply a source of prestige for the galleries and an inexpensive show for the museum. In the first

Lausanne exhibition, the Galerie Svensky-Franska, for instance, showed the work of Wols and Yves Klein. The most that could be claimed, however, is that this gallery had been the first to show them in Sweden, for the artists were already exhibited elsewhere by that time. Thus the exhibition is a form of concealed advertising, but one likely to impress gallery clients unfamiliar with the facts.

The position of the Bienal de São Paulo is more complex. The exhibition space is like an abandoned factory, and the location, out of town, is unknown to most of the residents; the exhibition is attended only by people directly engaged in the operation. It is not, in the full sense of the word, a public exhibition at all; it is more like a convention in a remote place. Of course, the prize can be a desirable episode in an artist's ascending career, and the catalogues are circulated as evidence of the show's having taken place. As an exhibition, however, it is a kind of fiction with extensions into reality in the form of catalogues and prizes. What the catalogue can amount to is shown by the 165-page book published by the National Collection of Fine Arts on the occasion of the 9th Bienal.[3] Harold Rosenberg, who attended the opening of the 6th, has recorded its disorganization and lack of substantial art. He lumps together "the São Paulo and Venice biennials,"[4] but the comparison is absurd. It serves, in fact, to underline the accessibility of Venice, the solidity of the organization, and the high calibre of some of the exhibitions as well as of the total effect, which is, often, a profile of current trends.

The Biennale as a Structure

The status of the Biennale, founded in 1895 by the City of Venice, was fixed by a law of December 24, 1928, N. 3229, in which the exhibition was declared an autonomous agency (*ente autonomo*). The Agency was to provide the organization that previously had been the responsibility of the city, and the city was to hand over the exhibition buildings. The financing was to be provided by the Government, the City of Venice, and the profits of the exhibition (admissions, commission on sales, catalogue receipts).[5] The law, signed by Vittorio Emanuele III and Mussolini, directed that a five-man commission be appointed to administer the Agency. It was a typical piece of Fascist reorganization aimed at greater efficiency, and it worked.

The commission's President was Giuseppe Volpi di Misurata, and he turned out to be the right man, in some respects, to preserve the stability of the organization. For one thing, he had ties of friendship with the organizers and artists of the early Biennale, such as Riccardo Selvatico, Antonio Fradeletto, and Ettore Tito, although the phase of taste that they represented was played out by the 20's. That Volpi accepted a traditionalist view of painting and sculpture is clear from the exhibitions during his administration. Under Fascism the range of the Biennale as an international affair diminished as a tough Italian nationalism gained confidence. However, Volpi increased the scope of the Biennale by expanding into other arts. In 1930 a biennial, then annual, Music Festival began, and in 1932 a "Convegno di Poesia" (which awarded a prize to Giuseppe Ungaretti), but it did not survive a second meeting in 1934. The great success of the expansion of the Biennale was the Mostra Internazionale d'Arte Cinematografica in 1932. The cultural benefits to Italy, the conversion of so many professionals into tourists or tourist-attractions, and, maybe, the patriotism expressed in the Italian art in the Biennale itself, led to official recognition of the Agency's importance. A Royal Decree of 1938 allocated additional funds and sanctioned the position of Volpi and Antonio Maraini, the Secretary General. The structure of the Biennale, whether run by the City or as a separate Agency, remained constant: massive Italian coverage at the center of autonomous national exhibitions. This form, susceptible of drastic changes of content, has proved capable of absorbing cultural and political shifts without damage to the stability of the exhibition.

The Pavilions

The pavilions in the Giardini, where the exhibition is housed, are erected by each country and the styles are a vivid array of national self-images. As the pavilions are occasional architecture, they are more demonstrative than buildings put up for continuous use; they are frivolous, but sensitive to the cultures from which they originate. At a large exhibition, the total effect, the sum of the physical plant and its content of individual works, has a meaning. To look only for the pure art content within the circus of material display at large-scale shows confuses this meaning. Such an approach leads to a constant antagonism between the containing system and the exhibits contained. The exhibition itself, as we shall argue later, has a structure, and hence a message, as much as the art that it shows. Here we can approach the architecture as a model of nonverbal communication, somewhat like an exhibition. The pavilions, built and rebuilt at various times, can be divided into categories of folkloric, classicizing, and international. The Hungarian pavilion is folkloric, with a monumental Art Nouveau Romanesque door, encrusted with four-star folk art; so is the Soviet pavilion, with dormer windows and bulging ornament, like a product of Western influence on conservative Slavic workmen. The Greek pavilion has a facade on the lines of a Byzantine basilica, with patterned brick that makes the surface look like Harris tweed. Equally folkloric is the pseudo-classicism of the Central Pavilion facade and the Italian-designed galleries across the Canal di Sant'Elena, which house Roumania, the U.A.R. (or R.A.U. in Italy), Yugoslavia. Flattened columns without capitals, empty niches, shallow curves: this is the streamlined classicism of official Fascist architecture, rhetorical but austere. The big portico with square columns and pinched entrance steps of the German pavilion is in the Nazi version of the style.

The classical styles are all highly indicative of their countries. Across from the Olympic Games classicism of the German pavilion is the post-Petit Trianon French pavilion, with a portico on an oval plan and delicate detailing. Between these two buildings is the British pavilion, with high steps up to a wide loggia, where bricks and white columns raise instant memories of Georgian style. It looks like an Italianate English country house. The American pavilion, with its tiny dome and miniature symmetrical wings, is Colonial neoclassic, halfway between Monticello and Howard Johnson. The Danish pavilion is a sharp and austere neoclassic revival building, a reminder that Thorwaldsen has a museum dedicated to him in Copenhagen. International style shows in various forms: the Spanish pavilion, self-contained in solid walls, has a Frank Lloyd Wright look, as does the Swiss pavilion, long and low, with factory-studio windows ranged above. Later forms of international style are shown by Japan's pavilion, a dizzy bit of cantilevering entered through the *piloti,* and by Brazil's, a glass and wood box entered by a jutting concrete tunnel. Canada has built an intricate wigwam of glass and wood around a tree, presumably to symbolize love of nature. In truth, perhaps all the pavilions are, to some extent, folkloric.

Organization and Influence

In discussing an exhibition as large as the Biennale, and as important, it is necessary to confront the rumors and suspicions that are triggered every two years. The selection of the artists and the awarding of the prizes are, of course, the sensitive areas. That the choice of artists can be problematic is shown by the recent history of the United States pavilion, but the problems are administrative tangles, well within the power struggles normal to institutions. The American pavilion is now sponsored by the National Collection of Fine Arts in the Smithsonian Institution, Washington; it decides on the museums to be invited to arrange Government-backed art shows. In 1966 the invitation was issued to the Guggenheim Museum in New York and later withdrawn. According to the curator of international exhibitions in Washington: "The proposals they have finally submitted would involve expense of such magnitude that we could not undertake at this late date to raise the funds for it." [6] In 1968 an invitation was issued to the Los Angeles County Museum for Venice and then withdrawn, too. According to David Scott, director of the N.C.F.A.: "Los Angeles' was an interesting proposal but it came late and when it did it wasn't worked out enough. On the other hand, the Geske proposal fit cleanly into our budgetary requirements." [7]

In both cases, lateness and expense are cited because they are inarguable and tolerably polite reasons. (There was a diversion in the case of Los Angeles when Edward Kienholz, a protest assemblagist included in the proposed list of artists, was rumored to be the reason for Washington's withdrawal, but he was not.) Scott said, a bit airily: "I frankly don't remember whether Kienholz was in the Los Angeles proposal . . . I know they had lots of trouble over his show in Los Angeles last year, but that sort of thing never bothers us." [8] The argument about expense is doubtful, but the lateness is unquestionable. In both cases the delay originated with the directors of the respective museums, T. M. Messer at the Guggenheim, Kenneth Donahue at the County Museum. To quote *The New York Times*: "It is known that the Guggenheim delayed the final submission of its proposals to the government agency until after an initial choice by its curator, Lawrence Alloway, had been overruled by the museum's director, Mr. Messer. When the National Collection tapped the Guggenheim to do the show last December, it was generally assumed that the choice had been made specially with Mr. Alloway in mind." [9] Similarly with the Los Angeles museum; it was assumed that it received the invitation so that Maurice Tuchman, curator of modern art, would arrange the exhibition. Hopefully, the N.C.F.A. has learned enough about American museums not to try in the future to get curators, when the official invitations have to go to the institution, that is, to the director. As for Messer and Donahue, they share the unusual distinction of being museum directors who have lost the Venice Biennale for their museums.

What about all the intrigue and corruption that are supposed to surround the prizes at Venice? The press is full of unsupported allegations, such as: "Leo Castelli, Mr. Lichtenstein's New York dealer and the man generally credited with 'arranging' the prize for Robert Rauschenberg two years ago . . ."[10] This was written by Hilton Kramer before the prize winners were announced in 1966, and Lichtenstein did not get one. What, precisely, was the alleged "arrangement" has never been told, and it was apparently unrepeatable two years later. The Rauschenberg success was something of a surprise, to his dealer as to others, whereas Lichtenstein's chances were somewhat optimistically viewed, by his dealer and others. To quote Kramer again: "Certainly the campaign for Mr. Lichtenstein seems well organized. The bookshops here [in Venice] are prominently displaying a bright and hastily produced illustrated multilingual paperback anthology of critical writing on Mr. Lichtenstein's work . . . Three international art journals featuring Mr. Lichtenstein on their covers . . . are very much in evidence, as is a fourth, *Art International,* published in Switzerland by an American. The last contains an article on Mr. Lichtenstein by Otto Hahn, the French critic, and has nothing about the other Americans showing here."[11]

The point that is not made by the writer is that all this activity is out in the open and cannot fairly be linked to the implied corruption of an "arrangement." The interest in Lichtenstein did not culminate in a prize (reportedly the French juror François Mathéy vetoed moves in this direction). The prize winner, for once, caused general astonishment: Julio Le Parc, Argentine kineticist, who was definitely getting his glory ahead of schedule. The trading that goes on in international committees, as a legitimate route to a consensus, promoted him accidentally. In the following year, the Stedelijk Museum, Amsterdam, originated a retrospective of Lichtenstein, undeterred by the artist's failure to hit the jackpot at Venice. Norman Reid, director of the Tate Gallery, London, was on the jury in Venice and seems not to have voted for Lichtenstein, but he accepted the Amsterdam exhibition for his museum. Prizes cannot be viewed in isolation, as sudden bounty; they are almost always part of a series of public events. It is noticeable that Louis and Noland, Olitski and Frankenthaler, in two successive Biennales, have interested Europeans very little, certainly less than Pop artists. The reason for this is not the inherent difficulty of the work, but is attributable, in part, to the amount of preparation by the artists' dealers. The Castelli Gallery artists, through the Ileana Sonnabend Gallery in Paris, have reached galleries, museums, collectors, in Europe. The artists of the André Emmerich Gallery, though shown in Paris at the Galerie Lawrence, had not reached a comparable point of European recognition.

The Biennale generates a mass of gossip, some garbled in the Giardini, some forgotten in Florian's. Gossip, entertaining as face-to-face communication, changes its meaning when it enters the press; here everybody's bad opinion of other people's activities is confirmed. Gossip is probably at a normal level for any comparable group, but the kind of group must be defined. Art dealing, which is a symbiote of the modern Biennale, is not a profession, in the sense that law, medicine, and architecture are professions. Internal self-regulation and the suppression of doubtful claimants are at a minimum. The Art Dealers Association of America, more concerned with raising the image of the business than with regulating it, resembles the self-bestowing prestige organizations of the television and movie industries. The profits and the risks of art dealing are both great; dealers are free to improvise on a basis of personal ingenuity in ways that members of a profession cannot. There is a connection to the garment business and selling carpets which art dealing has not yet lost.

This situation does not make unfounded hints about "arrangements" any more credible: flattery, perhaps—but bribery, unlikely. The jurors, who are usually distinguished men, at least in their own countries, have too much to lose, and so have ambitious dealers. Influence is exerted in another way. It is more economical to shift the focus of the art-oriented communications network than to buy somebody. The way to reach a juror is the same way that the dealer influences the collector and the public, by taking advertisements and supplying color transparencies to journals, encouraging critics, lending to museums, cutting prices for collectors, and so on. The kind of underground activity implied by Kramer is a primitive conception; the media are the route to the juror's attention, as to yours and mine. The operation is thus in the open to an extent that people prone to conspiracy-theories of events or who revere the idea of that old-time payoff find hard to believe.

The Future of the Biennale

Umbro Apollonio, Curator of the Historical Archives of Contemporary Art, in conversation with me, speculated on the Agency's role. He stressed that he was sharing personal thoughts, not implying policy. He pointed out that in 1968 it was becoming necessary for the Biennale to do more than be informative. The massive presentation of great numbers of works from different countries is the foundation of the show. This function of data-assembling had been the proper course after World War II, but he regarded it as basically fulfilled. The dealers, who after the war had been slow to reorient themselves to an altered art scene, were now a highly effective force in the art world. Museums all over the world, too, showed recent art in quantity, he pointed out. Possibly the prizes, which once served as a stimulus to artists, might no longer be effective in their present form. Few big international shows with a prize system had smooth prize-givings any longer. He was amused at Asger Jorn's dramatic telegram rejecting a Guggenheim International Award in 1964. I reminded him of Henry Geldzahler's attack, as Commissioner of the American pavilion, on the principle of the jury system at Venice. These were extreme examples of a general attitude, he considered. If the prize system were modified it would be possible, he hoped, to structure the exhibition around governing ideas. Today, the general knowledge of modern art, greater than it has ever been, was ready to support thematic and ideological shows. (Incidental support for this view is the shift towards informative catalogues by the National Collection of Fine Arts in their Biennale plans.) At present the Biennale is formed, as always, by the participating countries' send-ins, over which Venice has no say, and by random conglomerations on the labyrinthine walls of the Central Pavilion. What is necessary now is to discover a means to confer order on the thick samples of present activity.

The Biennale as a Party

If you visit the Biennale on the day it opens to the public, it feels as if it has just closed—one or two tourists and students, some nuns (if the Patriarch has not forbidden the exhibition), and a few sailors (if the Italian Navy is using the port facilities). It is the four days of the official opening that give the Biennale a special value; here are more artists, dealers, collectors, and writers in one place at one time than can be found anywhere else in the world. Each nation gives a press party and there are other fringe benefits and entertainments. Rosalind Constable described the hectic preview period as "part vernissage, part horse race" [12] when she covered the 1962 revels. This was Hundertwasser's big year, and she describes him as "a tall, slim, unsmiling man of thirty-three, with a red fringe beard, who invariably wore a black art-velvet jacket and was accompanied by his beautiful young Japanese wife, in Japanese dress . . . Collectors and dealers quickly beat a path to the door of the Austrian pavilion to buy him, or sign him up." [13] Recently, American collectors have given prizes with their names on them (David E. Bright was the first, followed by, for instance, Robert C. Scull). Others give parties, such as the one staged by Arnold A. Maremont, manufacturer of automobile parts and a respected collector, for 130 people. They "boarded a *vaporetto* at the Hotel Cipriani" for a trip to Torcello; then back to the Cipriani for "a Lucullan feast." [14] Apart from the fact that people in the same business are usually congenial, the Biennale is an arena for making or renewing contacts, arranging shows, monographs, sales, visits, articles. There are, too, the people who openly use the event for publicity, like Hundertwasser, or Harold Stevenson, who was not in the Biennale but a beneficiary of the crowded scene. Rosalind Constable described him as "a *fin-de-siècle* young man from Idabel, Oklahoma . . . generally dressed from head to foot in white . . ." "A new Michelangelo. I adore him,"[15] his dealer Iris Clert was quoted as saying. She rented a palazzo and hung banners: "Iris Clert, Piccola Biennale." The rest of this book is about the big one.

The Biennale as a Target

1968 was not a great year either for parties or for developing solutions to any of the Biennale's problems; both activities were pointlessly interrupted. Venetian students, cued by student activism elsewhere in the early summer, demonstrated against the Biennale and succeeded in closing it briefly and in postponing the awarding of prizes. Biennale officials, as sensitive as the students to the high level of student dissent, closed the exhibition after the official opening. When it reopened the Giardini were crowded with police. Estimates put the number of students as low as a hundred and as high as five hundred, but, in fact, Umbro Apollonio estimates that between two and three hundred students (eighteen to twenty-three years old) were involved.[16]

Some news media reported the affair in terms of the iconography of a global student conspiracy. According to *Newsweek,* "The Venice Biennale reeled under relentless blows of students from Italy and France *converging* (my italics) on the city of canals."[17] According to *Time,* "Revolution-minded students from Madrid, Paris, and other points began deplaning in Venice."[18] Foreign students were deplaning and more were detraining all summer long in Venice, but, in fact, they were not central in harrassing the Biennale.

Most of the students were from the Accademia di Belle Arti, hardly famed as a center of student unrest and rebellion (as, say, the University of Caracas is). Several months before the

Biennale opened students began protesting their conservative training. By the time of the opening of the Biennale, they had already seized studios at the Accademia. Thus the Biennale was an incidental target for the students, though an inevitable one since it coincided with their action.

On June 7th, less than two weeks before Biennale's opening, a manifesto against the exhibition was published, signed by "the committee of students, workers, and revolutionary intellectuals to boycott the Biennale." [19] "The 18th June, the day of the vernissage, the day of the cultural market, we must all be present, workmen, students, intellectuals, united in the struggle against capital, against the bosses, against bourgeois society." [20] The student manifesto, headed "Workmen, Companions," attacked the Biennale as "one of the moments in which is concretized the mechanism of repression and mystification of the culture of the bosses" (padroni). The Biennale is, that is to say, contaminated by the historical context of declining capitalism from which it emerged. The art and organization of the Biennale are both attacked for appealing to merely "a limited number of people." In fact, the Biennale and other big exhibitions function to take art out of an elite context, but this fact is not amenable to the simplistic drama of the manifesto. One of the reasons given for the boycott is that "through Venice the Biennale represents an essential moment in the articulation of a tourist activity destined for the rich . . . And it enriches the great hotel companies together with the big industries which exploit our labor." [21] The statement is decidedly archaic, with its sociologically ignorant division of Venice into an alliance of dissenting students and Venetian workers *v.* rich visitors. (No doubt such resentments arise in any tourist city where most of the inhabitants exist economically at a level far below that of the tourists.)

Actual disturbances were lightweight: placards and painted slogans, small groups outside the American pavilion shouting anti-U.S. slogans, a clash with the police in the Piazza di San Marco. One poster stated: "Dopo la Pop-Art . . . Poliz Art." At one level this touches on notions of workers against strikebreaking police, but it also touches on the more generalized, and more recent, hostility to the police felt by all students, housewives, pacifists, and sub-groups engaged in public protest. Referring to the police guard in the Giardino this poster also included a reference, typical of many, to the first "Esposizione Internazionale di Polizia." Another poster, with a brutal hand holding a truncheon, carried the words: "For the First Time in the World the Exhibition Is the Police! XXXIV Biennale." [22]

A theme-show, in the Giardini but arranged independently of the national pavilions, surveying the art of 1950-65, had been scheduled. This exhibition, a moderate but welcome first move towards another form of exhibition than one based on national identity, was cancelled: the alarm caused by the demonstration thus weakened the first real effort to reform the exhibition system, a step that even the students had been demanding. [23] Fear of vandalism to expensive foreign works led not only to this cancellation, but to postponement of the Biennale prizes. Prize-winning works would have been obvious, perhaps irresistible, focal points for further protest, assured in advance as they were of excellent coverage by the media.

Insurgency is the style of direct action at a time when democratic institutions have been stereotyped and poorly administered. The Biennale was reportedly attacked as "bourgeois" and "capitalist." One placard read: "The Biggest and Worst Exhibition in the Biennale Is the Police," and another described the exhibition as "the Biennale of the Bosses." The continual references heard to Marx, Mao, and Che Guevara (or students shouting "Ho Chi Minh," outside the American pavilion) were probably less political than individualistic, for in Italy a communist vocabulary provides what is, fundamentally, the only common language of dissent. Whereas formerly the communists were skilled at making opportunistic use of the local forms of discontent, the position is now reversed. Communist iconography has been appropriated for use as the signal of individual revolt. Marx and Lenin are ambiguously separated from the form of society that actually embodies their ideas, the U.S.S.R. The language of dissenting students in the United States and often in Europe, though frequently derived from the theory and history of insurgent warfare, is not, with any consistency, communist.

One gesture of international support for the students came from Denmark, in the form of a single-sheet leaflet, rather like the students' original statement. It was headed, "Declaration For Our Italian Artists and Comerads [*sic*]: Follow Courbet" and signed "Jens Jørgen Thorsen, Caesar, Jørgen Nash" (Asger Jørn's brother). "An iron-ring of police is now defending the exhibition-area. We thank you, Italian comerads [*sic*], for your deed! It has shown that the terror-police by all means is defending the art-police." Here is an example of shreds of communist rhetoric used to affirm a purely artistic kinship.

Various artists reacted sympathetically to the students, often on the basis of freedom and anti-institutionalism: at least fifteen Italian artists withdrew their work, as did three French artists and one each from Sweden, Denmark, and Yugoslavia. It was an opportunity for them to show kinship with the young, as well as to express some of the resentment they felt about the existing system of merchandising their wares, in which the Biennale plays a prominent role. Artists feel caught, as indeed they are, with no available alternative to dealers' galleries, museum exhibitions, and international shows.

Reports of student demonstrations and riots, mainly in New York and Paris but also in Belgrade, must surely have acted as an incentive to the Venetian students (not traditionally resolute) and undoubtedly were a source of apprehension to the Biennale officials, leading them to exaggerate the vulnerability of the Biennale to what was, in the event, very little pressure for a very short time. (The students' manifesto included the sentence, "France instructs," referring, of course, to the student uprising in Paris.) The possibility of tourism's being adversely affected by a real confrontation of students and police was no doubt worrying, and close at hand was the sobering example of the Triennale in Milan, an industrial design exhibition and conference which had been prevented from opening at all by a student sit-in supported by artists.

The communications media that disseminate reports of demonstrations and riots today must be reckoned as a major contributing factor to similar events. There is an immense amount of "inside" information concerning their manipulation; this example is typical: "The crowds don't just happen. 'People have no idea how much behind-the-scenes work goes into a spontaneous demonstration,' says a Rockefeller advance man." [24] In fact, an increasing number of people have a very clear idea, with the result that middle-class students have learned the pessimism long known to the poor and underprivileged. "Passaic is decaying and all we get from the politicians are promises," [25] says a housewife trapped in a New Jersey town. Conversely, the students, at Columbia and at Venice, know how easy it is to use the media that have contributed to their disillusionment. Thus in Venice the presence of the Biennale conferred the status of major news on what was a minor rebellion compared to those in New York and Paris, and the Biennale was not even the initial target of the demonstration.

When an artist sees his work in the Biennale he may feel trapped in the circuit of the art world, and also experience other discontents. He may feel ambivalent about the gaudier aspects of the scene he is entering. There is, too, a kind of temporal vertigo. At a big, recurrent exhibition, you have a sense of recent art behind what you are looking at now and a sense of the next art, not in form but in sequential order, on the way in. Artists concerned with the uniqueness of their own work or critics anxious to stabilize taste at a certain point are understandably oppressed by this sense of time like a production line. Of course, being shown at Venice is a sign of recognition, but, at the same time, it is a recognition of age. Hence the belief of the Abstract Expressionist generation that retrospectives are only for the young.

1. "Official Calendar for 1968 of the International and National Fairs and Exhibitions in Italy," *The Economist,* March 16, 1968.
2. Nikolaus Pevsner, *Academies of Art, Past and Present* (Cambridge, 1940).
3. São Paulo 9. United States of America, Exhibition catalogue, 1968. The expanded role of this catalogue by William Seitz and, to a lesser extent, of Walter Hopps' for the preceding São Paulo Bienal, typifies Washington's new requirements for catalogues, as only Alan Solomon's 1964 catalogue has done for the Venice Biennale. The intention is to produce well-documented and thoroughly-argued texts in place of the eulogistic puffs in past catalogues.
4. Harold Rosenberg, *The Anxious Object* (New York, 1964).
5. Constituzione della Biennale in Ente Autonomo, *Storia e Statistiche della Biennale di Venezia* (Venice, n.d. [1932]).
6. Quoted by Grace Glueck, "Guggenheim Loses U.S. Biennale Role," *The New York Times,* February 22, 1966.
7. Quoted by Grace Glueck, "Biennale, Bah," *The New York Times,* February 11, 1968.   8. *Ibid.*
9. Glueck, *op. cit., The New York Times,* February 22, 1966.
10. Hilton Kramer, "Art: Venice Machinations," *The New York Times,* June 16, 1966.   11. *Ibid.*
12. Rosalind Constable, "Part Vernissage, Part Horse Race," *Life International,* July 30, 1962.
13. *Ibid.*   14. *Ibid.*   15. *Ibid.*
16. Information supplied directly by Umbro Apollonio.
17. "Art. Venetian Carnival." *Newsweek,* July 1, 1968.
18. "Exhibitions. 'Violence Kills Culture'." *Time,* June 28, 1968.
19. "Operai, Compagni." Single-sheet pamphlet. Venice, 1968. The translations are by Ruth Ann Fredenthal, who helped me gather material on the student boycott.
20. *Ibid.*   21. *Ibid.*
22. Both posters are reproduced in *L'Ora,* Palermo, June 18, 1968.
23. Reform needs to take the form of reducing national sovereignty, on the lines of the large-scale *Documenta* exhibitions at Kassel, financed by the city, which are controlled completely by a central committee. The second *Documenta,* 1959, was the biggest coherent survey of post-war art seen up to that time in Europe, and the fourth, 1968, was an imposing sample of recent work, much of it by young artists.
24. "Smoothing the Way," *Wall Street Journal,* July 3, 1968.
25. "Passaic Debating Uncertain Future," *The New York Times,* July 8, 1968.

TWO

THE BIENNALE
AS SUPER-SALON
1895-1914

The silver anniversary of the marriage of King Umberto I and Queen Margherita of Savoy was the occasion for celebrations all over a newly-united Italy. On April 19th, 1893, the Municipality of Venice decided that their city's contributions should be humanitarian and cultural. Funds were set aside for an orphanage intended for the sons of shipwrecked sailors and Venetian workmen and for "a national biennial exhibition of art." These plans were arrived at three days before the actual date of the anniversary and the exhibition was scheduled to open one year later, but in fact the opening did not take place until 1895. This is not surprising, since the organization of a big exhibition is complex and demanding, involving communication with scattered people and the creation of an efficient control system. Their Majesties attended the opening of the exhibition on April 30th, 1895, thus celebrating their silver wedding anniversary in retrospect (fig. 5).

An official Commission was established, consisting of prominent citizens and artists born or resident in Venice.[1] It was decided that the exhibition should be primarily invitational, but with provision for other artists to submit their work to a jury. Here one detects the influence of the artists' discussions at the Café Florian which preceded announcement of the exhibition. It was decided, too, that the exhibition be, not national, as was first proposed, but international in scope. The send-in by uninvited artists was later dropped, but the decision to include foreign art was of central importance. It is the source of the exhibition's greatest strength in its later development. The site chosen for the exhibition was the public garden, out beyond the mouth of the Grand Canal, on the way to the Lido. The area had been reclaimed from the Adriatic during the Napoleonic occupation and was, in 1893, in use as a public garden, with an elephant named Toni for children to ride, and stables for cavalry horses. The presence of cavalry in a city of canals is an attractive idea, but progress, in the then-modern form of a great exhibition, triumphed.

A subcommittee was set up to implement the Commission's decisions on policy. Consisting of local artists, it was headed by Enrico Castelnuovo (sculptor); the members were Bartolomeo Bezzi (painter), Marius De Maria (known as "Marius Pictor"), Antonio Fradeletto (who was to serve as Secretary General for the first eleven Biennales), Giuseppe Minio (engineer), Emilio Marsili (sculptor), and Augusto Sézanne (painter). Fradeletto consulted by mail eminent Italian and foreign artists about the desirability of the proposed exhibition and was reassured by a very favorable response. Growing out of these informal contacts a Committee of Patronage was formed of the major official artists of the time, whose works, as we shall see, dominated the early exhibitions.

As usual when discussing committee decisions, even those made within the intricate structure of city administration, an individual emerges as decisive; in this case it is the Syndic of Venice, Riccardo Selvatico. The position is equivalent to that of mayor, and he seems to have been an administrator with a strong feeling for Venice's internationalism; but then, how many mayors have been poets? When he announced the exhibition publicly, he declared it would represent "the most noble activities of the modern spirit without distinction of country." There is no doubt that he meant this and was not merely exercising the rhetoric of public occasions. He remained available for consultation throughout the planning stages and, as we shall see, firmly resisted the Patriarch of Venice (later Pope Pius X), who suggested the removal of a controversial picture from the first Biennale. (This was the first of three known attempts at religious censorship; the Pope himself intervened in 1930 and a later Patriarch in 1964.) The other sustaining figure was

Antonio Fradeletto, the critic, who, as Secretary General, worked from an improvised office in the Library of the Commune. He, with Giovanni Bordiga, looked after all the correspondence, preparation of the catalogue, and such details as the special tickets which included round-trip rail fares and admission to the exhibition. Fradeletto was assisted by a Working Committee (*comitato ordinatore*) of artists, five of them carried over from the original Commission: Bartolomeo Bezzi, Antonio Dal Zotto, Pietro Fragiacomo, Emilio Marsili, and Augusto Sézanne. Bezzi, Marsili, and Sézanne had been on the subcommittee as well; the new members were Guglielmo Ciardi, Luigi Nono, Ettore Tito, and Alessandro Zezzos. Their esthetics, and their actual production, are conspicuous in the early Biennales.

It is only recently that Munich's importance in the nineteenth century has been acknowledged again in the history of art in which the primary position had been pre-empted by Paris. It was, for example, in Munich's international exhibitions that Bezzi found a model for the Biennale regulations. There were international art shows in the Munich *Glaspalast* in 1886 and 1888. The latter, *Der III Internationalen Kunstausstellung,* was presented as a hundred-year jubilee, because of an art exhibition, an exceptionally early one, in the city in 1788. The catalogue of the jubilee lists 2,732 modern works, divided by media, and a historical section one eighth the size of the modern, divided into the "Eras" of Karl Theodorus, Max Joseph I, and King Ludwig I. Though German and Austrian artists were preponderant, the show was legitimately an international affair, including such artists as Arnold Böcklin, G. Ciardi, Walter Crane, Carolus-Duran, Giacomo Favretto, Hubert von Herkomer, Max Liebermann, and Ettore Tito. That is to say, a comparable stratum of taste was displayed at Munich and Venice.

Bezzi proposed that the Venice exhibition consist of generally recognized Italian artists, invited foreign artists of repute, and a limited number of uninvited but juried works. The Commission, in accepting Bezzi's formula, aimed for one hundred and fifty paintings by invited Italian artists, the same number by the invited foreigners, and a selection of fifty from the send-in. These

figures were instantly exceeded; the first exhibition actually included 516 works, nearly three-fifths by foreign artists.

The regulations governing the Biennale, as set out in the
first catalogue, are a model of logistic requirements for big
shows. A few details will indicate the thoroughness of the
planning: invited artists could submit, with no expense for
packing and transport, two works of up to three meters in the
main dimension (painting) and four hundred kilos in weight
(sculpture); exceptions were to be negotiated in advance. Uninvited artists had to bear packing and transport expenses, but
if accepted there was no unpacking and repacking charge in
Venice. Strong wooden cases, whose tops should be closed only
with screws, were specified. If a work were sold the Biennale
was to receive ten per cent, and if a conflict occurred between
a sale made through the Working Committee and a sale made
privately by the artist, the artist must yield. The percentage from
sales of exhibited works has been an important part of the
funding of this chronically underfinanced exhibition. Typical
of the economies with which it has always been administered is
the facade of the exhibition building erected in the winter of
1894-95 (fig. 1). It was in gesso, and with the Venetian climate
and neglect in off-years, it was under constant repair for the
twenty years that it stood. (The facade, designed by the artist
Marius De Maria, was replaced in 1914 by another gesso facade
of equal vulnerability by Guido Cirilli [fig. 2].) This limited
expenditure might be compared with costs of some of the special buildings erected for the World's Columbian Exposition in
Chicago in 1893: the fireproof Palace of Fine Arts cost
$670,000, and even the reproduction of the Convent of La
Rubida (where Columbus retreated) cost $50,000—and these
were but two of a multitude of buildings.

There is, however, one sense in which the Venice and Chicago
exhibitions can be compared. It has been customary to admire
the contributions of engineers to exhibition architecture (such
as the Eiffel Tower, built for the 1889 Paris Exposition) and
to dismiss the buildings erected as revivalist architecture. Both
Venice, with its single building, and Chicago, with its miniature

city, eschewed engineering solutions. The Palazzo dell'Esposizione, as De Maria designed it, was one of the least Venetian buildings in the city. It was ultimately Roman in its Beaux-Arts use of classical orders and sculpture occupying niches, pediment, and roof. It was, also, set in a tree-filled park, well away from the water; the minor canal which crosses the exhibition ground, the Canal di Sant'Elena, is masked from view for the most part. It is, essentially, a park of French or Roman style, and as such, is conspicuous in an environment of waterfront buildings and a maze of canals. This element of estrangement operated, also, at the Chicago fair, where elaborate waterways were built from Lake Michigan to the site. The buildings were mainly classically inspired and built in a shining white plaster derivative which led to the exhibition's being called the White City, as the glass structure of Joseph Paxton in London gave rise to the name Crystal Palace. This cluster of buildings in the Midwest, an array of domes, deep porticos, giant orders, open pavilions, loggias, and obelisks, all close to a waterline only a few steps below the bases of the buildings, is irresistibly reminiscent of Claude's and Turner's paintings of ideal port scenes. This realization in three dimensions of the visionary landscape of painters produces a subtle play with paradoxes of monumentality and expendability, art and commerce, Claude in Illinois, Rome in Venice.

The form of Venice's tribute to *Umberto il Buono,* that of a major compilation of art, links it to a series of nineteenth-century prestige-exhibitions. To appreciate the character of the Venetian institution, including aspects of its subsequent development, it is useful to relate the Biennale to the growth of annual art exhibitions in Europe. The French Salon, which began biennial exhibitions in 1737, and the English Royal Academy, founded in 1768, led a proliferation of exhibiting societies. At these exhibitions, art, unmediated by church or monarchy, was seen without time-lag by a large audience, far bigger than any earlier group given access to uncommissioned, freely-invented art. The public exhibition of art, by quantifying what had previously been restricted by and to elite patronage, was an important factor in the democratization of art. Here began, in fact, the tension that still exists between systems for the wide distribution of art and an esthetic that rests on the concept of an elite minority.

The Biennale, by reason of its size, needs to be related also to the giant nineteenth-century exhibitions in which art from all countries was combined with technology and science. This was the usual form of prestige-exhibitions, of which early examples are the Great Exhibition in London, 1851, and the Exposition Universelle in Paris, 1855. An exhibition is, it must be stressed, ideological in form, a sign-system that is more than the sum of the separate exhibits that it contains. An exhibition is not an aggregation of things that can be inspected separately. T. S. R. Boase, for example, summarized the Prince Consort's view of the implications of the 1851 exhibition, for which he was largely responsible, as "free trade, division of labor, increase in means of communications, the stimulus of competition." [2] The English Prime Minister Gladstone, anticipating the World's Columbian Exposition in 1893, expressed this position exactly. He voiced the hope that "the Chicago Exhibition would materially advance commercial intercourse between nations, and therewith, the sentiments of friendship." [3] It seems clear that the monster show was in itself a celebration of the new logistic and industrial capacity of the nineteenth century. The optimism of the last century which underlies such a world-view is now largely in doubt. Modern critics of big exhibitions are more likely to agree with John Ruskin's verdict on the Great Exhibition: "The populace of England rolls by to weary itself in the great bazaar of Kensington, little thinking that a day will come when those veiled vestals and prancing amazons, and goodly merchandize of precious stones and gold, will all be forgotten as though they had not been." [4] The fact that much of the art and crafts of the exhibition has seemed bizarre and irrelevant for several generations gives only superficial support to Ruskin.

In 1854 the Crystal Palace, the prefabricated structure that had housed the Great Exhibition, was reassembled on a new site. The commissioners of the forthcoming Paris Exposition Universelle of 1855 were invited to the opening, but as Delacroix, one of the commissioners, records, almost nobody accepted.[5] Although engaged on a similar enterprise he regarded the 1851 exhibition as merely the ostentatious evidence of affluent commercial power. From our viewpoint, however, both exhibitions seem related episodes in the tremendous expansion of global contact in the nineteenth century and the acquisition of a new sense of scale. Baudelaire, who reviewed the Exposition Universelle at length, had a brilliant sense of this modern factor to which Delacroix, his senior by more than twenty years, was not alert. Baudelaire's article is best known for his agonistic opposition of Ingres and Delacroix, but the first section, dealing with the effect on the spectator of big exhibitions, is far more illuminating:

> There can be few occupations so interesting, so attractive, so full of surprises and revelations for a critic, a dreamer whose mind is given to generalization as well as to the study of details—or, to put it even better, to the idea of universal order and hierarchy—as a comparison of the nations and their respective products.

He modifies the word "hierarchy" immediately:

> All I wish to do here is to assert their *equal* utility in the eyes of Him who is indefinable, and the miraculous way in which they come to one another's aid in the harmony of the universe.

He addresses the reader, exhorting him:

> ... imagine a modern Winckelmann (we are full of them; the nations overflow with them; they are the idols of the lazy). What would *he* say, if faced with a product of China— something weird, strange, distorted in form, intense in color, and sometimes delicate to the point of evanescence?

And yet such a thing is a specimen of universal beauty . . . Few men have the divine grace
of cosmopolitanism in its entirety.[6]

Here is a clear statement of the impact of great exhibitions on
the nineteenth century. There is the confrontation of Winckelmann with nonclassical culture and the coexistence of known
Greek-derived forms with unfamiliar ones. The world may be
shrinking, but a "cosmopolitan" sensibility must expand to
meet it. A big exhibition is a compressed journey, the journey
to the Orient or to Africa, taken by the exhibition visitor in
the course of a single day. Perhaps the earliest example of a
massive congregation of mixed art took place in Paris in the
summer of 1802, when Napoleon's cultural loot was displayed
in the Grande Galerie of the Louvre. Contemporary comment
included the complaint that there were too many works to be
seen comfortably and coherently. Critics of modern exhibitions,
unable to adapt to the experience of compressed or instantaneous
travel, still repeat this complaint. Their anxiety at runaway
abundance undermines the pleasures of plenty.

To deal organizationally with such abundance requires the
well-organized setting of goals and schedules and logistic efficiency on an international scale. That is to say, the exhibition
has to work like an industrial or military operation. To deal
perceptually with such simultaneity and quantity requires of the
spectator, as Baudelaire points out, a post-classical sensibility,
one trained to cope with the plurality of styles and objects available to industrialized man. Exhibitions are propaganda, not only
for our transformed sense of scale, but for specific projects, mer-
cantile in the case of the Great Exhibition, tourist in the case
of the Venice Biennale. The *Palazzo* dell'Esposizione, as it was
symptomatically called, was a contribution to tourism, a palace
for the people, as well as an addition to the European exhibition
schedule. The inclusion of foreign artists' works was an inducement to foreign visitors, of course, far greater than a purely
Italian art show would have been.

Until the eighteenth century, writing about art tended to be in the forms of either technical manuals or biographies, but with the emergence of public exhibitions another form of discourse became possible. Critics, as they can now be called, wrote promptly on current shows and their opinions could be measured against the latest works themselves. This has been, in fact, the basis of art criticism since Diderot's *Salons* (1759-81); it is still the custom to take big exhibitions as the occasion for a special effort. The Biennale has been continually an occasion for critics to put forward, from their national viewpoints, synoptic think-pieces, surveys of the "art of our time," analyses of the "cultural crisis." Although writers have been the beneficiaries of the big shows, at Venice and elsewhere, there has been little attention paid to the exhibition as a form in itself. Throughout the Biennales, incidentally, national newspapers (which restrict Biennale news to announcements of their country's representatives and prize winners, if any) and critical journals (which customarily scrutinize the art of the country in which the journal is published) are equally parochial. French publications give French news, American give American news, and so on.

Big exhibitions are artificial environments, somewhere between carnivals and museums. They are dependent, of course, on the mobility of works of art, as they are taken from original sites and permanent repositories with a freedom equal to that with which a critic selects photographs for reproduction. In this respect, a recurring exhibition like the Biennale is more like the drive-in movie theater than the museum from which some of its exhibits may be borrowed. It is *originals* that are being spun around the world, and so to speak, inserted, into a core of permanent services at the exhibition ground. The particular relation of scale and facture, experienced only in the presence of the original work of art, is preserved, but in contexts that can change as fast as conversation. These contextual shifts have meant that works of art acquire additional comparative meanings as their company changes. The theoretical absoluteness of art has been modified by the mobility of art in successive man-made environments.

The Biennale must also be considered in terms of education, not only of the public but of Italian artists. In the 1901 catalogue, for instance, the hope is expressed that the show would be "educational for our artists," a theme that Alessandro Stella, writing around 1912, elaborated. He pointed out Italian art's dependence on foreign examples and deplored the consequent time-lag, which he estimated at twenty years.[7] If it was a purpose of the Biennale to rescue Italian art from what Mario Praz has called its "peripheral character"[8] in the nineteenth century, it was not soon achieved. The Venetian artists most closely engaged with the exhibition, from discussions at Florian's to various roles in committee, were precisely the ones who shaped Italy's peripheral artistic culture. The Biennale had no influence on speeding up the development of an internationalist outlook among Italian artists, because for the first period of its existence the art shown generally confirmed the existing taste for the work of men like Ettore Tito and Pietro Fragiacomo, Giacomo Favretto, and Guglielmo Ciardi. The Biennale from 1895 until 1914 (when it was suspended because of World War I) was, in fact, devoted to the celebration of official European art. As such, it was a medium of consolidation, not of expansion (or education).

The Committee of Patronage[9] was formed with the tactical function of providing the authority of High Art to the new Biennale. It included Michael Munkacsy, a then-famous artist of the Austro-Hungarian Empire, which was at that time, nationally, a strong force in bravura academic painting; P. Kröyer from Denmark (fig. 20), Carolus-Duran from France, Lord Leighton from England, and eight Italians, among them Francesco Paolo Michetti (who turned out to be the first-prize winner of the first Biennale). Half the Committee had been born in the 1820's and 30's, and only two of them, Joaquin Sorolla from Spain and Anders Zorn from Sweden, were born as late as the early 1860's. The members of the Working Committee, who selected from the send-in, were attuned to this stratum of taste without scepticism or reserve. It cannot be said that the Biennale was started without the greatest regard for the artists themselves, but it can be thought that the artists themselves were opportunistic and inflexible.

It is easy to forget how early communications between countries accelerated. As an example, the Exposition Universelle of 1855, which included a special room for Théodore Rousseau, also exhibited works by the English Pre-Raphaelite Brotherhood, representing another kind of naturalism than that of Rousseau and the Barbizon School. It is worth recording that the Brotherhood had been formed in London only seven years earlier and was at first generally attacked; given the prudence of committee decisions and the organizational problems of big exhibitions, this represents a minimum time-lag. Holman Hunt and John Millais (represented by *The Order of Release*) were both shown. By comparison with such speed, the Venice Biennale, granting its commitment to various forms of naturalism, appears unadventurous.

Bates Lowry has pointed out that the academic artists of the 1880's have been isolated from their historical situation and rejected automatically in the twentieth century: "By this condemnation," he observes, "modern critics have enabled the 'melodrama' of modern art to enjoy a continuous run." [10] We have also, by reflex, committed ourselves to a monolithic definition of art which limits our attention to a comparatively restricted style-range. To reach an understanding of the earlier Biennales, and of the world-wide situation it reflects, academic art needs to be looked at again. Achille Fould, who was an organizer of the Exposition Universelle, addressed the prize winners of the 1857 Salon in these terms: "Poetry, morality, religion, history—those divine wellsprings where the masters found inspiration—have in no way run dry for their successors." [11] Here is a concise statement of the idealizing trend that characterized ambitious Salon art until the 1880's. However, it is false to reduce the situation in late nineteenth century Europe to a clash of idealizing academic artists and naturalistic moderns, as is constantly done. On the contrary, later academic art is characterized by forms of realism and by an irrevocable corrosion of all those classicizing elements praised by Fould.

(As a matter of fact, in the period between World Wars I and II, that is, from the 12th to the 23rd Biennale, modern art and classicism are affiliated in ironic forms that we shall trace later.)

The relation of the artists we call modern and those we call academic cannot be resolved here, but something of the real complexity of history, as opposed to the simplicities of "melo-drama," can be indicated. Connections exist within the supposed antagonism. Velasquez, as rediscovered by Manet, is a crucial point in the formulation of the theory of "a modern sensibility" as proposed by Ortega y Gasset and André Malraux. Velasquez, was, with Franz Hals, also the model for Carolus-Duran, the society portraitist and Salon artist from whom J. S. Sargent learned his rapidity of execution. Sargent ("academic") knew Monet ("modern") and visited him at Giverney a few years before being elected Associate of the Royal Academy, London. Bouguereau, though a Salon hero, was admired by Van Gogh. It has been pointed out [12] that eighteenth-century elements can be detected in the Barbizon School and eighteenth-century re-vival forms were important in academic painting (indeed, they were a source of anti-idealist elements). They are present also in Sargent's *Acheson Sisters* (fig. 58), in which a group of girls round an urn simulates a composition by Sir Joshua Reynolds. Jozef Israels, much respected in early Biennales (fig. 57), was also admired by Van Gogh. Possibly Israels' Rembrandtesque slurring had a special appeal to a fellow Dutchman, but Van Gogh was not alone. Israels was generally admired for "the nervous vigor of an untaught hand," and, to quote a contempo-rary, "Israels laughs a little at *la belle peinture.*" [13] Here, then, we have to account for an academic painter indifferent to *la belle peinture,* which is hard to do in terms of a simplistic mod-ern/academic polarity. The work of an artist like Domenico Morelli, who combined discursive subject matter (exotic or Christian) with painterly ripple and fatness, was regarded in his own time as a "union of the realistic and academic meth-ods." [14] To view Morelli now purely as an academic artist is to impose a retroactive simplicity on history's real data.

The character of international Salon art as refracted, with a strong Italian emphasis, at the early Biennales, is both non-idealizing and nonaristocratic. The boundaries of history pictures (noble subjects from the Bible, classical culture, or the lives of the saints) and genre scenes (views of everyday life) were dissolved. History was treated intimately in terms of its anecdotal quality and everyday scenes could be treated with the concentration and on the scale once reserved for historical subjects. A naturalistic, nonheroic view of the world is expressed by Salon iconography. Mario Praz's characterization of Italian Romanticism is apposite: "good-natured fun," "the steady cult of a sane, clear-sighted observation of human destinies, mixed with humor and pathos," and "homely themes, humble folk, a studied simplicity." [15] The shared assumption of a majority of later Salon artists is of an art that does not need special knowledge, but rests on the verities of common experience. The human heart replaces the humanist's library. Some titles, not typical but exaggerated, from the 1897 Biennale will clarify a kind of subject matter now absorbed by the mass media: *Torturing Suspense (During the Operation of a dear person); A Halt on the March of Banished Convicts in Siberia; The Mother (African Lioness and Cubs);* and *Courage Boys! Breton Fishermen (Finisterre).* Although not a prize winner, one of the most popular paintings of the second Biennale, in that it was most widely reproduced in the press, was Repin's *The Duel.* It depicts the moment after the shots have been exchanged and the regretful winner extends his hand to the respected, dying loser, a pathetic moment-of-repose after violence. This art of immediate appeal, exclusive of prior knowledge or intellectual difficulty, might be called post-elite art. It is an art of reduced esthetic distance, direct in its attraction for the spectator, whether in terms of subject matter or sensual appeal (as in virtuoso handling of oil or bronze, or leaving much of the paper ground visible in a watercolor).

The first Biennale included works like Leighton's *Perseus and Andromeda* or Walter Crane's *Prometheus Liberated* (fig. 19), which were a continuation of the idealistic grand manner of early Salon art. These works were conservative and less characteristic of the official taste of the time than were departures from this classicizing norm towards a variously embodied naturalism. Nudes, for example, tended to be treated with an undercurrent, or indeed at times an outward show, of eroticism. Ettore Tito, a constant exhibitor in the early exhibitions, showed in 1895 a painting entitled *La Fortuna*. Instead of a figure relatable to the slim, chaste symbol that crowns the Dogana, at the end of the Guidecca, he showed, in steep perspective, a very plump flying nude, heaving the wheel of Fortune around. The Venetian humorous paper *Sir Tonin* picked up the image and accurately turned it into a wildly gross study of buttocks. Traditional iconography, derived from the Renaissance, becomes in such pictures a perfunctory screen for the show of skin. Hence, these paintings, and contemporary sculptures, contributed to the devaluation of the intellectual, idealist element of earlier academic art. Tito's *The Pearl* (fig. 23), of almost twenty years later, is milder, but in the absence of an iconographic program, the girl becomes to some extent intimate in pose and participative in appeal. When mythology is retained, it is frequently ostentatiously erotic, as in the work of Giulio Aristide Sartorio and Gaston La Touche (figs. 46, 52).

Plein-air landscape was common, without the conventions of studio-constructed paintings, but equally without the amorphous dazzle of fully-developed French Impressionism. In fact, French Impressionism, as it evolved in Monet's late work, or as it stressed increasingly the physiognomy of the paint, led away from its naturalistic origins towards abstraction.[16] German and Italian Impressionism either retained a basis in Courbet's monochromatic solidity or imposed design as a source of order on shifting color. French Impressionism is not, therefore, a relevant norm for the judgment of all European and American plein-air painting of the last third of the nineteenth century. In the Biennales the general emphasis was on the open air as a real place, with changing light-effects, though moderated by dark tonality or linear construction. These landscapes have a humble, but not revolutionary, cast of peasants, farmers, and girls. Scenes of low life, derived originally from mid-century

Naturalism but with eighteenth-century pastoral modifications, are common: the spectrum runs from Israels' emanations of mud and clay to Morelli's or Michetti's ripe girls of the people. That this stylistic range did not shift significantly until 1920 can be seen from the prize winners between 1895 and 1914 (figs. 42-60).

Michetti's *The Daughter of Jorio* (fig. 42), the prize-winning painting of 1895, curiously displays the non-epic ambition of a sophisticated Salon artist of the time. The origin of the work was a journey in the Abruzzi that Michetti made with Gabriele D'Annunzio. They observed that adults in the region were "still known in patriarchal manner, not by their own names but merely as son or daughter of their father," [17] and one name they heard was "la figlia di Jorio." D'Annunzio wrote "a pastoral tragedy" of this title, with mingled themes of passion and superstition. Michetti painted a large canvas with life-size figures, but without D'Annunzio's tragic grandeur. Michetti's daughter of Jorio strides past a frieze of reclining males who react with various displays of Latin psychology. She hides her face from them and the spectator sees only her nose and mouth. The question "Who is she?" becomes the spectator's equivalent of the sexual attention of her audience in the painting.

After Michetti's first prize of 10,000 lire there were five 5,000-lire prizes, distributed as follows: Giovanni Segantini, Max Liebermann, Julius Paulsen, Domenico Trentacoste, Silvio Rotta; one prize for Venetians only was divided among Ettore Tito, Cesare Laurenti, and Alessandro Milesi. One prize of 2,500 lire was awarded to James McNeill Whistler for *Giovanetta Bianca* (fig. 10), or *The Little White Girl.* The jury consisted of William Michael Rossetti (Dante Gabriel's brother), Julius Lange, Richard Munthe, Robert de la Siseranne, and Adolfo Venturi. The prizes to Segantini, Liebermann, and Whistler are ratified, so to speak, by subsequent history (at least this far), but most of the early Biennale prize winners are strangers to posterity. The ratio of Italian to foreign artists among prize winners is high, given the large numbers of invited foreign artists; this is a recurrent problem in later Biennales, too, in opposition to their declared internationalism. On the other hand, perhaps we should really respect the members of the first jury for being right three out of fourteen times.

There was also in 1895 a "Premio Popolare (par referendum)" and the public voted for Giacomo Grosso's *Il Supremo Convegno* (fig. 9). Around an open coffin five nude girls climb or loll, scattering flower petals, in a "last rendezvous" with some monument of *machismo*. The Don Juan implication, the proximity of death and sex, created a scandal that prompted the Patriarch of Venice to express to Selvatico, the Syndic, his concern about the rumor of a work in the exhibition "highly offensive to the morals of the people." He requested the painting be withdrawn. Selvatico moved fast and invited the well-regarded writer Antonio Fogazzaro to consider the work and discuss the problem with his Commission. They concluded that the work would not damage public morality, and on this basis Selvatico defended the Biennale against church pressure. The Patriarch remained unsatisfied and the picture remained in the exhibition. This problem is one that plagued the spread of universal education and the wider distribution of works of art. The more people have access to a work, the more does censorship become attractive, both to bureaucratic administrators and to well-intentioned critics, ready to decide for a public actually grown beyond any simple canon of censorship. All the "democratic" media have been, in turn, the subject of minority anxieties: the moral effect of the novel in the eighteenth century; the sensationalism of magazines in the nineteenth century; the limits of sexual tolerance in films recently; and, part of this cluster, the contents of public exhibitions. The scandal, however, of Grosso's painting was irresistible, and *Il Supremo Convegno* was purchased by Venice Art and Company for a tour of cities in the United States, but the unrepressed painting was totally destroyed in a warehouse fire before the tour started.

As early as 1899 the awards were changed to acquisition prizes, which meant that the honored works were kept and deposited in the Galleria d'Arte Moderna in Venice (and sometimes in Rome). The move was a sound one in terms of the city's interests, taken in the belief that Venice would, in this way, build up an important permanent collection of modern art. In addition, the organizers of the Biennale presumably felt secure that the success of the exhibition was so great that it would be safe to economize in this area without losing the interest of artists. (Originally the prizes were high to attract artists of international reputation.) The acquisition policy was continued in 1901, and has been reinstated sporadically since, but in 1903 a more drastic economy was made. In this year, and until 1907, gold medals inscribed "Gran Premio della Città di Venezia" were issued in lieu of cash. In 1909, 1910, and 1912 the Municipality acquired half a dozen works for the museum from each show, and in 1910 a new prize was instituted, the Premio Dreber. In 1914 the number of prizes had risen to three; then World War I ended the whole matter for a time. Despite the financial pressure these wavering awards suggest, a sign of the confidence and energy of the organizers is the decision they made when faced by the prospect of clashing with a huge Esposizione Internazionale di Bella Arte in Rome in 1911. They advanced the 9th Biennale a year and held it in 1910, rather than postpone it until 1912, as a less competitive administration might have done. (Since then, the Biennale has always been held in even-numbered years.)

It is too easy to deride the first eleven Biennales as a super-salon. Given the initial connection with Munich, for instance, a bias towards realistic representation is to be expected, and it is legitimate. During the period 1895-1914 it would be unreasonable to expect "peripheral" Italy, not yet accustomed to French Impressionism, to show German Expressionists and French Cubists.[18] There is, however, a legitimate complaint, one that is valid in terms of the choices historically conceivable for Venetians of the period. Thus Werner Haftmann has been misled by his expectation to describe the early Biennales as disclosing "the sweeping influence of European symbolism,"[19] but this is not, in fact, the case. The complex of Symbolism—Art Nouveau—Jugendstil—Stilé liberté—is curiously underrepresented at Venice. The original Committee of

Patronage included, it is true, Puvis de Chavannes, Gustave
Moreau, and Edward Burne-Jones, who might have steered the
exhibition towards a Symbolist position, but they were over-
whelmed by artists representative of Salon taste. This situation
is manifest in the exhibitions: for example, in 1899 there were
works by Klimt, Whistler, Hodler, Khnopff, and Jef Leempoels
(figs. 14, 15), but these were only a few works scattered in an
alien context. It was not until 1910 that Klimt was given a
one-man show (fig. 21). Thus the related currents of flatness
and allusive subject matter were present as a very tentatively
stated alternative to the abundant, but actually declining, Salon
art. One early exception was in the Biennale of 1901, in which
Rodin showed twenty works, including the Balzac monument.

That the possibility of showing Art Nouveau in some form
existed, but was not realized, can be seen by two special exhibitions in 1897 and 1899. The first of these was a Japanese
exhibition of pure and applied art; the second was *Scottish Decorative Arts,* including designs by Charles Mackintosh for a
Glasgow tearoom, and works by his wife and his sister-in-law,
Margaret Macdonald and Frances E. Macdonald.[20] With modern
Japanese design and the most sophisticated of all Art Nouveau
represented in successive Biennales, one might expect interest
in this style to increase. There was, in addition, though not available to the public, a suite of galleries for the press in elegant
Art Nouveau style.[21] At first it would seem that the Venetian
tradition of craft would find the new style congenial, but in
fact the conservatism of Venetian decorative crafts blocked its
acceptance. Interest in the decorative arts was very strong among
the Biennale's organizers, as can be seen from the galleries devoted to the different regions of Italy, but they were committed
to luxuriance and historicism. Take the Emilian Gallery, 1903
(fig. 17), which was decorated by a Bolognese group: the walls
are divided horizontally, the upper area carrying polychrome
trees and flowers by Achille Casanova, alternating with relief
sculptures of girls by Giuseppe Romagnoli; the ceiling was
painted by Sézanne, who also designed the hanging, gilt electric
lamps. He was responsible, too, for an ornate mirror frame

which carried down into the lower wall some of the ebullient ornament of the upper area. The Venetian Gallery was equally profuse and included a frieze painted by Fragiacomo of the sails and pennants of galleons, viewed from below against what was described as a sky of quiet green. Aside from these regional showcases, other galleries carried massive furniture and oddities such as the ornate ceramic bench with a great overhang in the Gallery of Modern Portraits at the 1903 Biennale (fig. 18).

The example of the Italian decorators was followed later by both France and England. The French decorated their pavilion with a painted glass ceiling by Paul-Albert Besnard, which reconciled, if that is the word, the leanness of the Pantheon decorations in Paris with Venetian ceiling design. Frank Brangwyn, halfway between a kind of historicist Baroque and a muscular Art Nouveau, filled the British pavilion with friezes, over the doors and round the walls. The mingling of built-in decorative art and compact easel painting was partly the result of a desire for synthesis, a rich unity of the arts and architecture, and partly the prolongation of Salon presentation style. The ambitious exhibitions of the later nineteenth century not only included elaborately framed paintings and sculptures mounted on pedestals, but ornamented walls, fountains, indoors plants, and elaborate furniture (figs. 11, 19). The heavy frames, which are obtrusive and seem to act as barriers to the pictures they contain when viewed today in comparatively bare display spaces, were once ingredients in a total fusion aimed to delight the senses. It should be noted, on the other hand, that the Biennale always adhered to one-line hanging, not only in the ornate chambers where there was no room for anything else, but in the undecorated rooms also. The decision not to rank works one above another was reached at an early point in the planning.

Fradeletto was interested in the coordination of art and architecture and, as Secretary General, was in a position to advance it. His lack of sympathy for Art Nouveau may be deduced from the decorative schemes that he supported. In 1907 G. A. Sartorio painted a "poem of human life," a series of panels which

were descendants of Raphael's grotesques. These detailed alle-
gories were regarded by Fradeletto as substituting for the small
works and objets d'art that the conditions of a big exhibition
excluded. Thus, their function was to infiltrate and fill up rooms
which would otherwise have had uninflected areas. In 1909
Fradeletto had Galileo Chini decorate the cupola of the first
gallery in the exhibition building with scenes of the history of
art: primitive, Greek and Roman, Byzantine, Renaissance, Michelangelo, The Empire of the Baroque, and the New Civilization. (This commission led to another: the decoration by Chini
of the King of Siam's Throne Room.) Finally, in 1912, Pieretto
Bianco decorated a gallery with proto-Fascist work-imagery; the
artist referred to the "inspiration of arduous labor" as he balanced massed workmen on scaffolding, with the domes of St.
Mark's in the distance. The ambitious scope of these decorations
reveals a nostalgia for the iconographical programs of humanism. This searching for intellectual content is unlike the main
direction of Salon art. The high seriousness of the star works
of earlier Salons had been modified by the late nineteenth century and its extension, sometimes called *Fine-ottocento* (meaning art done in the twentieth century in the spirit of the
preceding century).

Something of what the Biennale might have been architec-
turally, without the commitment of Fradeletto and Venetian
artists to post-Renaissance craft traditions, can be seen by reference to the first *Exposizione Internazionale d'Arte Decorativa
Moderna* in Turin in 1902.[22] It was opened by the young King
Vittorio Emanuele III, King Umberto having been assassinated
by an anarchist two years before. Here were environments by
Mackintosh and the Glasgow School, by the German Peter
Behrens, the Belgian Victor Horta, J. Herbert McNair from
Liverpool, and others. It was a spectacular show of every shade
of Art Nouveau, whose verve makes one aware of the heavi-
ness of styles at the Super-Salon on the Lagoon. Responsibility
for the esthetic character of the Biennale is not wholly Venetian,
but must be shared to some extent by the national committees
who became responsible for administering the emerging na-

tional pavilions. No doubt each country accepted the lead of Biennale policy, but even so, the level of independent discussion was low. Typical is the English subcommittee of 1910 (a working group implementing a large committee's directives): George Henry, A.R.A., R.S.A.; Thomas Grosvenor, R.S.W.; and Francis Derwent Wood, A.R.A. English artists are unique in the Biennale catalogues for keeping all honors that carry any initials or titles with them, but it is their only distinction.

The central exhibition building consists of connected rooms, in flexible sequence. The layout of the exhibition in 1897 is characteristic of how the space was used. The visitor who more or less followed the galleries from A to V would have seen the following displays: Turning left, after entering, one saw the work of twenty Belgians, followed by two galleries of mixed international art; then four Italian galleries, but with a Spanish section in one, and Norwegian and Swedish entries in another. The art of Norway (again), Denmark, and Russia was housed in a gallery that led into another international room. The Japanese exhibition followed, succeeded by a group of international etchings, with a special section on the Dutch. American art shared one room with British and one with French art. Scotland had a room of its own, Austria-Hungary (thirteen artists) shared with Germany; Germany also had a room of its own, as did Holland. Thus the exhibition was compounded of (1) an international mix, (2) geopolitical groups (Austro-Hungarian Empire and Germany, or the "Sala del Nord," as a German, Russian, Scandinavian group was called in 1901) and (3) national units. The spectator's progress through the exhibition, his intergallery movement, was, therefore, an analogue of nineteenth-century internationalism. Gradually, however, the predominant character of the exhibition changed, with the appointment of special commissioners to prepare national or theme shows. This led to a progressively stronger emphasis on national identity in later Biennales.

The character of the exhibition changed in another way, too; originally each artist was represented by one or two works, but increasingly the Biennale stressed one-man shows. In this respect, though perhaps in no other, Hubert von Herkomer, the British painter, was a pioneer; he had a one-man show in the first Biennale and his was the only one. In 1897, the year of the second Biennale, Rodin was represented by five plasters, and Wilhelm Leibl, a leading painter of the Munich realists, by seven works. In 1899 the Venetian painter Giacomo Favretto, who had died in 1887, was given a retrospective, a precedent of prime importance for the future (fig. 12), while Michetti and Franz von Lenbach (Munich, again) had one-man shows. Among the early theme shows, two held in 1899 were of French landscapists "della scuola del '30" (Corot and the Barbizon School) and "American Artists in Paris." During the remaining Biennales before 1914, one-man, thematic, and regional exhibitions increased (representatives of the different regions of Italy having been added in 1901 to the existing committees). An interesting project was the Gallery of Modern Portraits, a survey of the possibilities of combining painterly succulence and descriptive solidity (fig. 18). Boldini, Carolus-Duran, Carrière, Lavery, Lenbach, Sargent, Whistler, and Zorn were among the artists represented.

The success of the Biennale can be seen in the attendance figures, the number of works exhibited, and the number of works sold, all of which advanced impressively between 1895 and 1912 (see *Appendix*). There were minor setbacks in 1914, the year in which World War I violated the highly developed international culture which then existed. Incidentally, the Syndic Selvatico was President of only the first Biennale; from 1897 until 1920 this office was filled by the Syndic Filippo Grimani. Until 1914 the Secretary General was Fradeletto. In 1903, Romolo Bazzoni was named Head of Administration, a post which he held until 1942. (In fact, sixty years after his original appointment, he wrote a book on the Biennale.[23]) An index of the Biennale's importance is the appearance in the Giardini of national pavilions to supplement the previously lone Palazzo dell'Esposizione. The first was the Belgian in 1907, followed in time for the 1909 exhibition by the Hungarian, British, and German pavilions. For 1912 Sweden built a pavilion next to the Belgian, and France a pavilion opposite Germany's. A Russian pavilion was ready for 1914. The layout of the gardens assumed a form which has been amplified, but not structurally changed, by all the later pavilions. In 1914 the Belgian pavilion showed the works of James Ensor and Theo van Rysselberghe; the Central Pavilion gave one-man shows to Federico Zandomeneghi and Medardo Rosso. Ironically, Neo-Impressionism, in the person of van Rysselberghe and Zandomeneghi, was accepted before representative French Impressionist paintings had been seen at Venice. The Biennale was starting to shift from its protracted allegiance to late Salon art to a moderate admission of extra-Salon art. The tendency had begun in 1910 with one-man shows of Monticelli, Renoir, Courbet, and Klimt, waned somewhat in 1912, and was revived in the following Biennale, which was to be the last for six years.

1. The full membership of the Commission was: Bartolomeo Bezzi, Antonio Dal Zotto, Marius de Maria, Antonio Fradeletto, Pietro Fragiacomo, Michelangelo Guggenheim, Cesare Laurenti, Marco Levi, Emilio Marsilo, Giuseppe Minio, Nicolo Papadopoli, Augusto Sézanne, Giovanni Stucky.

2. T. S. R. Boase, *English Art 1800-1870* (Oxford University Press, 1959).

3. Quoted from *Harper's Monthly,* 1892, by Betsey Goldberg, *The Chicago World's Columbian Exposition: The Contemporary Point of View,* unpublished paper, Skidmore College, 1963.

4. John Ruskin, *Modern Painters* (London, 1898 ed.), I, p. 454.

5. *The Journal of Eugène Delacroix,* trans. by Walter Pach (New York, 1961), entry for June 7, 1854.

6. Charles Baudelaire, "The Exposition Universelle," in *The Mirror of Art,* ed. and trans. by Jonathan Mayne (New York, 1956).

7. Alessandro Stella, *Chronistoria della Esposizione Internazionale d'arte della Città di Venezia 1895-1912* (Venice, n.d. [*ca.* 1912]).

8. Mario Praz, "Art and Letters in Italy," in *The 19th Century World,* ed. by Guy S. Metraux and Francois Crouzet (New York, 1963).

9. The full Comitato di Patrocinio is as follows: Michael Munkacsy, Ludwig Passini (Austria-Hungary); Charles van der Stappen (Belgium); P. S. Kröyer (Denmark); Puvis de Chavannes, Carolus-Duran, Gustave Moreau, Paul Dubois, J. J. Henner (France); Max Liebermann, Gustav Schönleber, Fritz von Uhde, Anton von Werner (Germany); L. Alma-Tadema, E. Burne-Jones, Lord Leighton, John Millais (England); Giovanni Boldini, Alberto Pasini, Cesare Dell'Acqua, Domenico Morelli, Giulio Monteverde, Filippo Carcano, Cesare Maccari, F. P. Michetti (Italy); J. Israels, H. W. Mesdag, J. H. L. de Haas, C. C. van Haanen (Holland); E. Pettersen (Norway); Ivan P. Pranishnikoff, L. Bernstamm (Russia, but resident in Paris); José Villegas, José Benlliure, J. J. Aranda, J. Sorolla (Spain); Anders Zorn (Sweden).

10. Bates Lowry, introduction to exhibition catalogue, *Muse or Ego,* Pomona College, 1963.

11. Quoted by Linda Nochlin, ed., *Realism and Tradition in Art, 1848-1900* (Englewood Cliffs, New Jersey, 1966).

12. Robert L. Herbert, *Barbizon Revisited* exhibition catalogue, Museum of Fine Arts, Boston, 1962.

13. Jan Veth, "Modern Dutch Art: the work of Jozef Israels." *Studio,* XXVI, No. 114 (1902).

14. Isabella M. Anderton, "The Art of Domenico Morelli." *Studio,* XXIV, No. 104 (1901). He is remembered, if at all, for a *Temptation of St. Anthony,* in which a psychologized saint rigidly tries

to ignore girls' faces in the painterly walls of his cave and a fleshy body rising from under a mat on the ground.

15. Praz, *op. cit.*

16. This point has been made familiar by recent American criticism of mid-century abstract painting. However, as early as 1931, A. E. Brinkman observed in "The Classical Temper of French Art" (*Formes,* XX [December, 1931]) that the trend of Impressionism was "anti-naturalist."

17. Charlotte Porter, introduction to Gabriele D'Annunzio, *The Daughter of Jorio* (Boston, 1907).

18. Ivana Mononi's thesis, *L'Orientamento del Gusto Moderno Attraverso le Biennali di Venezia* (Università degli Studi di Milano, 1956), examines the resistance to "modern" styles. (The substance of this thesis was published as *L'Orientamento del Gusto Attraverso le Biennali,* Milan, 1957.)

19. Werner Haftmann, *Painting in the Twentieth Century* (New York, 1965).

20. For a list of exhibits in this integrated environment, see Hugh Honour, "Biennales of Other Days: A Cautionary Tale," *Apollo,* LXXXIV, No. 53 (London, 1966). Another decorative possibility which was followed up elsewhere than at Venice was in the Russian pavilion in 1907: an exhibition organized by Serge Diaghilev included work by Leon Bakst and other modern designers.

21. Reproduced in *L'Art Décoratif,* LX (1903), pp. 85-89.

22. See *L'Exposition Internationale des Arts Décoratifs Modernes à Turin 1902,* ed. by Alexander Koch (Darmstadt, 1902).

23. Romolo Bazzoni, *60 Anni della Biennale di Venezia.* Preface by Rodolfo Palluchini (Venice, 1962).

HISTORICAL
PHOTOGRAPHS

1. Palazzo dell'Esposizione in 1895. Facade designed by Marius de Maria.

2. Palazzo dell'Esposizione in 1914. New facade designed by Guido Cirilli.

3. Palazzo dell'Esposizione. Facade in 1932, and as it appears at present, designed by Giulio Torres.

PRIMA ESPOSIZIONE INTERNAZIONALE D'ARTE DELLA CITTÀ DI VENEZIA · 1895

22 APRILE – 22 OTTOBRE

PREMI. MVNICIPIO L. 10.000 · MINISTERO L. 5.000 · PROVINCIA L. 5.000 · CASSA RISPARMIO L. 5.000

COMITATO DI **PATROCINIO.** AVSTRIA-VNGHERIA: Munkacsy· Passini – BELGIO : Van der Stappen – DANIMARCA: Kroyer – FRANCIA: Dubois· Carolus-Duran·Henner· G.Moreau·Puvis de Chavannes – GERMANIA: Liebermann· Schönleber·Uhde – INGHILTERRA: Alma Tadema · Burne Jones · Leighton · Millais· ITALIA : Boldini (residente a Parigi)· Carcano· Dall'Acqua (residente a Bruxelles)·Maccari·Michetti· Monteverde·Morelli· Pasini (residente a Parigi) – OLANDA : De Haas· Israels· H.W.Mesdag· Van Haanen – RVSSIA: Bernstamm – SPAGNA: Benlliure·Jimenez Aranda·Sorolla· Villegas – SVEZIA-NORVEGIA: Peterssen·Zorn·

PREM. STAB. C. FERRARI · VENEZIA

4. Poster of the First Biennale, 1895.
5. Their Majesties King Umberto I and Queen Margherita at the inauguration of the Biennale, 1895.

6. Il Duce at the Biennale, 1934.
7. Hitler at the Biennale, 1934, in the margins of a state visit to Mussolini.
8. His Majesty the King Emperor Vittorio Emanuele III (center), with F. T. Marinetti (right).

9. Giacomo Grosso. *The Last Meeting.*
1895.
10. James McNeill Whistler. *The Little
White Girl. Symphony in White, no. 11.*
Painted 1864, Biennale 1895.
11. International Gallery, D, at II Biennale, 1897. *The Flight of Charles the
Bold after the Battle of Morat,* by Eugene Burnand.

12. Giacomo Favretto, one-man exhibition, Gallery B, at III Biennale, 1899.

13. Giacomo Favretto. *Walk in the Piazzetta.* 1899.

14. Jef Leempoels (Belgium). *The Enigma.* 1899.

15. Fernand Khnopff. *The Sleeping Medusa.* Painted 1886, Biennale 1954 (Belgian Pavilion).

16. Tuscan Gallery, 1901. *Beethoven*, by Lionello Balestrieri (left). Committee for the decoration: R. Mazzanti, F. Gioli, V. Giustiniani, D. Trentacoste. **17.** Emilian Gallery, 1903. Decorations by A. Rubbiani, A. Sézanne, A. Tantarini, A. Casanova, G. Romagnoli.

18. Modern Portraits, Gallery P, 1903. Decorations by A. Tamburlini and R. Carbonaro. **19.** International Galleries, 33–34, 1907. *Garibaldi* by Plinio Nomellini (center), *John the Baptist* by Galileo Chini (tondo), and *Prometheus Liberated* by Walter Crane (right).

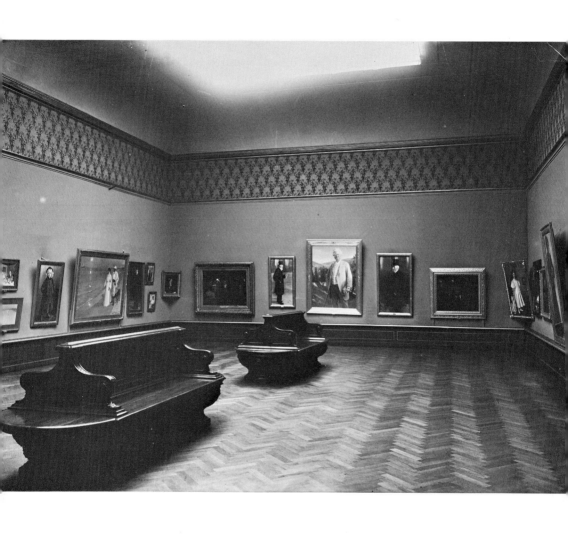

20. Peter Severin Kröyer, one-man exhibition, 1909.
21. Gustav Klimt, one-man exhibition, 1910.

22. Ettore Tito. *Le Rappezzatrici.* 1903.
23. Ettore Tito. *The Pearl.* 1914.
24. Pietro Fragiacomo. *L'Ora della Polenta.* 1924.
25. Alessandro Milesi. *Antonio Fradeletto.* 1935.

26. Gallery in the Central Pavilion, 1928.
27. Arturo Tosi. *The Track.* 1932.
28. Carlo Carrà. *The Bathers.* 1930.

29. Riccardo Schrotter. *The Judgment of Paris.* 1924.
30. Adolfo Wildt. *Il Duce* 1924.
31. Enrico Prampolini. *Mussolini: Plastic Synthesis.* 1926.

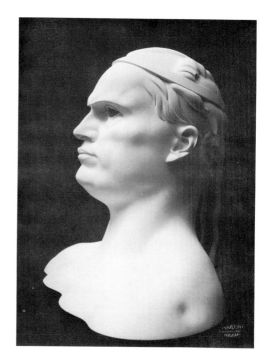

32. Postcard, 1930. The numerals XVII refer to the Biennale, and VIII to the Fascist calendar.
33. Postcard, 1940.
34. Futurist Gallery, 39, in the Central Pavilion, 1930.

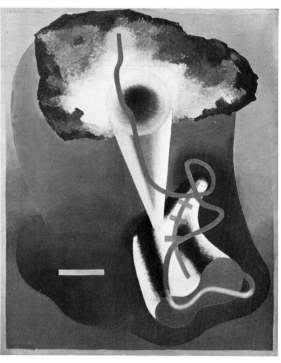

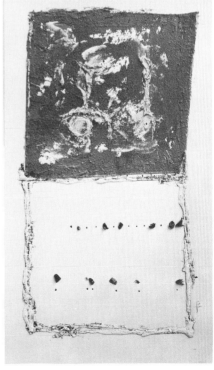

35. S. G. Tato. *Mechanical Splendor* (in the "Aeropittori Futuristi" exhibition). 1934.
36. Enrico Prampolini. *Inhabitant of the Stratosphere.* 1932.
37. Giuseppe Virgili. *Roman Civilization* (bas-relief). 1938.
38. Renato Guttuso. *The Execution of Nicola Belojannis.* 1952.
39. Lucio Fontana. *Spatial Concept.* 1958.

40. Roy Lichtenstein. *Temple of Apollo*. 1966. (Collection of Mr. and Mrs. Robert A. Rowan).
41. Ay-O. *Tactile Room*. 1966.

THREE

THE INSTABILITY
OF TASTE

What conclusions are to be drawn from looking back at the early phase of the Biennale? Can we, with the unearned gift of retroactive knowledge, treat the institution as a monument of the errors of an earlier generation? Such a view of the early Biennale as massively irrelevant has its temptations, to collectors with other interests, dealers occupied with other styles, and writers content with a simplistic view of history. I believe, however, that Biennales I to XI have a value considerably beyond that. The late Salon art in these exhibitions is not the product of a great style, but the exclusion of these artists has created a distorted view of recent art, producing an abbreviated view of human activity at a time of great abundance.

One of the problems is a great divisive idea stemming from the historical conditions of early twentieth-century artists, who out of necessity defined their work in opposition to its immediate alternatives. Thus the early writings of Kandinsky, Malevich, and Mondrian deal repeatedly with the differentiation, in absolute form, of their abstract art from realist and academic art. However, abstract art has been subject to several generations of later usage; artists have diversified, rejected, revised the premises of the early generation. Early modern artists undoubtedly experienced painful and unjust social pressures, but these conditions no longer exist. In terms of contemporary life the drama of Philistine versus Bohemian is archaic. The difficulty of new work can be a source of prestige rather than alienation; this is a period in which, to take two American examples, a thirty-eight-year-old painter can have a retrospective exhibition in a New York museum, and a thirty-two-year-old painter, generally recognized as avant-garde, is treated at unusual length in *Life* magazine.[1] This suggests that estrangement is no longer a constituent of modernism.

Modernism is not, obviously, an absolute; after all, the nineteenth and twentieth centuries provide us with numerous *old* modernists who are no more difficult of access than many of the new ones. Ortega was wrong to propose modern art as "essentially unpopular"; "the masses feel that the new art, which is the art of a privileged aristocracy of finer senses, endangers their rights."[2] Works of art do not possess modernity as an irreducible content. It is a time-bound concept, referring to original elements whose meaning can change in time. Art is subject to the learning process of the spectator which converts the unknown (in this case, new work) into the known and relates it to other ideas and objects. Thus a work of art's "modernity" is subject to erosion and disappearance. Incidentally, one of the sources of the modern-art-versus-the-public dispute was belief in the artist as genius, aristocratic in Ortega's sense; however much respect artists enjoy today, it does not, as a rule take this form of tribute. The artist is valued as a professional at least as much as he is as a seer. To compensate for the deflated cult of genius, therefore, supporters of modernism *qua* modernism have had to fall back on the idea of an art of inherent formal difficulty. Much of the traditional definition of modern art has been creator-oriented, to use Herbert J. Gans' term,[3] but creator-oriented criticism ignores the fact that art, to the audience, is a consumption experience in the sphere of leisure. Hence, ever-narrowing creator-oriented definitions of art have accompanied the expansion of society's ability to distribute and assimilate an increased diversity of styles. Art has become polarized between "modern" and "academic" styles, rather in the way that political democracy has been divided into liberal and conservative ideologies. However, just as this no longer provides the grounds for an accurate definition of the electorate, so the idea of two antagonistic taste blocs is too simple. Our society is not homogeneous, and it is an act of compulsion to assume that it can be contained by a single esthetic. Part of the value of the Biennale, in this context, is the way in which its past confronts us with suppressed traditions and forgotten artists.

Relativism in art is often regarded as the first step towards the collapse of all standards, towards an entropic sameness in which geniuses and hacks shall be indistinguishable. However, it offers the only way of allowing that everyone has allegiance to a cultural environment, or a taste culture, and that these differ. William Hogarth is an example of an artist caught between two cultural environments; his *desire* was for acceptance as a painter, but his *appeal* was as a print-maker, and the two media reached different audiences. Although the number of artists and the number of cultural environments have increased since the eighteenth century, esthetics and art criticism have become more dogmatic, monolithic, and exclusive. When we attempt to discuss art such as that shown in the early Biennales without prejudice, the limitations of present tolerance become very clear.

Aside from a simplified view of modernity, there is another factor which leads to an impoverished, though dramatic, view of recent art. Built-in to most histories of art since 1870 is a precipitous evolutionary view of events, in which Post-Impressionism replaces Impressionism, Cubism buries Fauvism, Op Art wipes out Pop Art. This view of art as a chain of successive movements, generating others in rapid sequence, has a depleting effect on our definition of culture. We lose a sense of the thickness of history, of its simultaneity, by accepting premature linear contours. It is not that artists and groups who have developed in this way are in any sense flawed by the line of inheritance. The limitation is in the writers and spectators who have failed to view the evolutionary elements in relation to other factors.

If we take taste to mean common perceptions and ideas concerning art, it seems clear that our field is marked by instability. The problem is compounded, but not created, by the difficulty of finding verbal equivalents for the sensory space of visual art. In the past, one of the standards of judgment derived from the artist's achievement of a convincing representation of forms in space. Judgment was a matter of balancing two kinds of knowl-edge, the subject and its translation, the referent and the sign. By the time of the early Biennales this rule was no longer un-failingly relevant in determining successful work. In the later nineteenth century, the free hand of the artist and the physiog-nomy of the art work itself as a visible factor introduced new problems. Estheticism and Impressionism solidified the work of art and reduced the references to external reality. Connoisseur-ship, with its interest in every artist's uniqueness of handling, weakened the grounds for comparative judgment between art-ists. It is interesting to note that the naturalistic tendencies of the Biennale provided ample license for painterly open-ness; paint as substance responsive to an autographic touch was as valued among Salon artists as among Impressionists.

The contrast of evolving modern art and inertial academic art, by which so many paintings and sculptures have been so simply evaluated, is too primitive a classificatory system. As we have indicated, late Salon art had its own historical dynamics. In addition, the schematic framework is alien to many of the artists that we are favorably viewing, as it were, from one side. For example, writers on Manet have supposed that his interest in exhibiting at the Salon, despite his connection with the Im-pressionists, reveals divided aims; Degas' lack of interest in the Impressionists' group exhibition has been misinterpreted, also, as further evidence of his misanthropy. These situations are perhaps problems only to the extent that they are posed in dual-istic form. If we accept the co-existence of Impressionism and the Salon, and of partial allegiance combined with impulses of withdrawal from Impressionists *as a group,* the problems seem more like human complexity than cultural conflicts. This is not to dissolve the grounds of stylistic differentiation, obviously; the danger does not lie here but in the reduction of an intricate and continuous history to a simple clash of opposites. Camille Pis-sarro warned Signac that Seurat was "of the Ecole des Beaux-Arts" [4] and therefore hazardous. It is understandable that Pis-sarro should feel like this about a younger contemporary who was, disconcertingly, both more traditional and more experimental than himself. To Pissarro the Beaux-Arts as a tradition was a threatening alternative to his own principles, but it is not a pressure on anybody now, certainly not in this form. What is interesting is the acceptance of both Impressionism and the Ecole des Beaux-Arts by Seurat in a logical and original synthesis of his own. The human complexity of the artists repeatedly exceeds the either-or choices of "modern" or "establishment" which our art history has proposed as their characteristic dilemma.

Modern art criticism and esthetics in the past century have been largely reductive in method. That is to say, art is simplified to one main tradition, one great school, one supreme moment, and other traditions are disparaged in relation to the degree of their departure from the norm. Art writing since Walter Pater is largely a lexicon of specialized arguments—for an art that is like music or like classical sculpture: for pure form, for social utility, for dream-imagery, for the record of process, for pure color—and each state is mutually exclusive. It is desirable when considering the Biennale to do more than complain about its omissions or deplore its departures from one or another of the easily available norms. It is true that the Biennale has missed opportunities, such as the early failure to offer hospitality to Art Nouveau, or, as we shall see, an overemphasis on classical-revival art between the wars. Such criticisms, however, are made bearing in mind the moves historically possible to the organizers at particular times; they attack failures of action, not departures from an ideal.

Perhaps it is now possible to consider an approach to the arts which does not assume the dominance of one line above all others, the centrality of one style compared to the marginal status of others. In fact, there is a perpetual decline and revival of individual artists, groups and periods. Rembrandt was in the process of being *rediscovered* as early as the mid-eighteenth century, but as a Fancy Painter of oddly-costumed characters. The Bolognese School of the seventeenth century suffered an early-twentieth-century eclipse and a mid-century revival, but the revival took a form that the nineteenth-century admirers of the school would hardly have recognized. These shifts in taste are part of a far more complex cultural situation than is usually admitted. The present, from one point of view, can be defined in terms of personal priorities; but it is, also, the pressure of coeval generations, overlapping as well as displacing one another. The present moment is marked by "the uncontemporary features of the contemporary"[5] (Wilhelm Pinder's phrase for the simultaneous presence of older and younger generations), as much as by clearly delineated major movements. It is not my intention to propose history as an enormous checklist of everything that happens, but it is necessary not to exclude too much, too soon.

What we have to deal with is the problem of point-of-view. A point of view is not stable with regard to a particular object or event, but subject to constant shift. We can distinguish, for instance, between at least three kinds of variables that affect our relationship to art: There are *personal variables,* by which is meant the difference between my opinion now and my opinion at another time. They account for such facts as that my second sight of a work is not the same as my first. *Individual variables* arise from the difference between the perception, interests, and memory of different individuals. Not only do these shift completely between one person and another, but we can never fully know the difference, which is locked in another person's experience. *Historical variables* are the products of general shifts of sensibility, such as the nineteenth century's rediscovery of Primitive Italian art after the indifference of the preceding three centuries. Ernst Cassirer has pointed out that "the truly great works of culture [have content] for us only by virtue of the fact that they must be continually possessed anew and hence continually recreated."[6] I cannot see why variability and renewal are a condition of great works only; indeed, with such changes going on, it is not certain that greatness, in this sense, is even a useful concept. Let us consider the position of Salon art as an example of the third variable, the historical. It had a facetious revival in France after World War II, at which time the eroticism of the iconography of bathers, robust mermaids, nymphs, and young witches on Walpurgis Night was relished. Salvador Dali treated academic art apart from its erotics, but his approach reduced the original material to the status of found material. There are signs of a revival now, both in terms of some neglected artists, such as Gérôme, and as a legitimate area of the continuum of art.

The art of the nineteenth and twentieth century has produced a situation of multiplicity that cannot be described by hierarchical and evolutionary schemes of order. A discussion of the Venice Biennale is, apart from anything else, a confrontation with historical density. Celebrity is no guarantee of historical fame, as the artists who were once praised and flattered at Biennales and are now forgotten testify. On the other hand, it is not inconceivable that some should be revived, a numerical factor which cannot be ignored. By the mid-nineteenth century the Paris Salon would, at times, receive 10,000 visitors a day to view the 5,000 or so exhibits: such plentitude of production and consumption continues. We are faced with a quantity of work and of spectators without precedent in history. The esthetics of elite and aristocratic art applied on this scale are irrelevant, though they continue to be viable, of course, as an individual variable. Meyer Schapiro has pointed to "the co-existence of an official-academic, a mass-commercial, and a freer avant-garde art. But more striking still is the enormous range of styles within the latter."[7] "The present diversity continues and intensifies a diversity already noticed in the preceding stages of our culture, including the Middle Ages and the Renaissance, which are held up as models of close integration."[8]

The diversity of style and iconography, even among the academic artists at Venice, is remarkable. Grosso's *Last Meeting* (fig. 9) is an image of death and sex, derived from genre scenes of parties. G. A. Sartorio deals with sex and death, too, but his painting celebrates the triumph of a fatal woman over the other sex (fig. 46) and his stylistic references are to the Grand Manner, though in terms of *fin-de-siècle* sensibility. In one sense, Whistler's *Little White Girl* (fig. 10) is a refined naturalistic portrait; at the same time, the Japanese detailing and the lassitude of the sitter relate the painting to another stream of nineteenth-century art. Derived from Ingres and Edward Burne-Jones, there is an iconography of static or sleeping women, as in Jef Leempoel's *Enigma* and Fernand Khnopff's *Sleeping Medusa.* The Leempoels figure addresses the spectator by a direct gaze, but is otherwise hieratic and passive (fig. 14), and the Medusa fuses themes of hybrid sexuality and sleep (fig. 15). These examples are from the comparatively meagre representation of Symbolism in the Biennale, and works like Giacomo Favretto's *Walk in the Piazzetta* (fig. 13) are more characteristic. As in the paintings of other genre artists who located their subjects in the past, there is an odd sense of time in his work; the scene is set in the eighteenth century and both the arcade of the Ducal Palace and the relaxed movement of people are recognizable; but whereas the Palace *endures,* the habits of people *recur.* Thus a hint of mortality is carried by the apparently inconsequential image.

Aside from the ambiguous elegiac mood, Favretto resembles other Venetian painters in his painterly style: his brushwork is reticent, but the paint deposit tends to buttery fullness. Pietro Fragiacomo, in *L'Ora della Polenta* (fig. 24), on the other hand, uses a dashing, semi-Impressionist facture to represent, as the title indicates, a characteristic time of day, lunch time, for the poor. Alessandro Milesi's *Marriage* (fig. 43) reveals an Impressionist relish of light and broken, moving surfaces, combined with a desire for the traditionally picturesque. In Lionello Balestrieri's *Beethoven* the music transports a listener, reminding us that great art and music in the nineteenth century were regarded as the trigger of Great Thoughts. Appropriately, in the installation photograph of the Tuscan Room, where Balestrieri's picture was hung (fig. 16), a suitably engrossed spectator is seated before the painting. The subject is a new one in art, drawing some of its drama from the romantic cult of genius. None of the topics mentioned in relation to these paintings has much currency in art criticism, but it is clearly inadequate that these works, and a multitude of others, be discounted without thought because they are neither modernist nor episodes in an evolutionary program.

1. Robert Rauschenberg at the Jewish Museum, New York, 1963; Frank Stella in *Life,* January 19, 1968. It is relevant to note here that *Time* and *Life* were in advance of the specialized art journals with information about Pop Art in the early 60's.

2. Ortega y Gasset, *The Dehumanization of Art,* trans. by Helene Weyl (Princeton, 1948).

3. Herbert J. Gans, "Popular Culture in America: Social Problem in a Mass Society or Social Asset in a Pluralist Society?" in *Social Problems: A Modern Approach,* ed. by Howard S. Becker (New York, 1966).

4. Quoted in Albert Boimé, "Seurat and Piero della Francesca," *Art Bulletin,* XLVII, No. 2 (1965). Boimé gives details concerning Charles Blanc's Musée des Copies, which deserves space in the history of museums and exhibitions as ideal environments. It was a plan for showing facsimiles of untransportable Italian Renaissance originals for the benefit of French students.

5. Quoted in Arnold Hauser, *The Philosophy of Art History* (London, 1959).

6. Ernst Cassirer, *The Logic of the Humanities,* trans. by Clarence Howe Smith (New Haven, 1966).

7. Meyer Schapiro, "Style," in *Aesthetics Today,* ed. by Morris Philipson (New York, 1961).

8. *Ibid.*

FOUR

THE BIENNALE
AND FASCISM
1920-42

The second phase of the Venice Biennale, 1920-42, is complex in terms of both Italian politics and European culture. There is a fundamental irony, or maybe incompatibility, in the spectacle of an exhibition predicated on international art in a period of increasing nationalism. Some of the constituent elements of Biennales XII to XXIII can be listed here and the effect of their inter-relations discussed subsequently. There is a conflict implicit in the fact that the rise of Fascism, which had an increasing influence on the Biennale, coincided with the first exhibitions of early modern art at Venice. In addition, the international style of Post-Impressionism was different in substance from the form of internationalism embodied in late Salon art. However, the Venetian artists whose taste shaped the early Biennales were not abandoned; they continued to be honored, but their painterly style was now accompanied by alternative forms of Italian art. There was programmed Fascist art as well as a subtle classicizing art not ostensibly Fascist at all. There was also a revival of Futurism which is oddly absent from the art history books in which "modern" art movements tend to be identified with progressive and revolutionary stances.

The term "fascism" has become as universal and vague a term of abuse as "communism," though not to the same group of people. One needs to remember that until Italy entered World War II on the side of Germany, Fascism was by no means universally distasteful. This is not the place for an embarrassing list of celebrities who admired Fascism, but to indicate, if possible, what the attraction was. One American reviewer of the 1930 Biennale, for instance, went out of her way to applaud

Fascism's vision and care for the arts.[1] The fact is, Fascism was the representative of competency of technique in government, and as such, was a European echo of American ideals of Technocracy. The saying that Mussolini made the trains run on schedule, outweighed, for a time, recognition of the brutality of his route to power. Fascism was "a movement for social renewal prompted by vague, passionate, and changing slogans," to quote Theodor Eschenburg, with "no political program but . . . a pseudo-historical fervor."[2] The nationalistic character of its fervor can be seen in its iconographical influence on art, but also in another form at the Biennale. Between 1895 and 1914, the sales of foreign works of art outnumbered the sales of Italian in seven of the eleven exhibitions. In the next twelve, however, only in the first year, 1920, did the sales of foreign art predominate. For the rest of the time, that is from 1922 to 1942, the sales of Italian work were overwhelming.

The Venetian artists who had done so well in pre-war Biennales continued to be visible, sometimes conspicuous: Bartolomeo Bezzi, Fragiacomo (a hundred paintings in 1924), Marius De Maria, were among the exhibiting artists; Ettore Tito showed in 1922, 1930, 1936, and 1940 (in date order, there were forty-two, forty-five, twenty-six, and twenty paintings). In 1932 twenty of the Venetian painters were celebrated in *Trent'anni d'arte Veneziana,* but elsewhere in the Central Pavilion was an inimical exhibition of Negro sculpture, the historically apt successor, in a Biennale that was beginning to show Expressionism,[3] to the Japanese exhibition in the Biennale of 1897. Also in 1932 Michetti, over a third of a century after he won the highest award in the first Biennale, showed thirty-two paintings. Giovanni Boldini, the dashing portrait painter, was given a large exhibition in 1932, and two of the new Futurists, Enrico Prampolini and Fortunato Depero, had one-man shows. In the British pavilion there was a show of Ambrose McEvoy, a hesitant and inhibited exponent of the Baroque revival that Boldini was lord and master of. The Biennale had become a more complex field of styles and taste than before.

This second phase of the Biennale begins with the arrival

of international modern art in Venice in quantity. There was still a time-lag, but an alternative tradition to that of late Salon art was adequately represented. The new administration of the Biennale (Giovanni Bordiga was President, Bazzoni continued as Administrative Director) included Vittorio Pica as Secretary General. He was a lawyer but did not practice, having turned to art and literary criticism; his taste was cosmopolitan (he was one of the first to promote Japanese art), but French-oriented. He popularized the Goncourt brothers, Zola, and Alphonse Daudet in Italy.[4] There can be no doubt that he was instrumental in developing the internationalism of the Biennales of the 20's. In 1920, there were one-man shows of Cézanne in the French pavilion and Archipenko in the Russian. In 1922, the Italian pavilion commemorated Modigliani, who had died two years earlier, and the French showed Bonnard, Maurice Denis (the leading theorist of the flat picture plane), and Emile Bernard (Cézanne's main correspondent). The exhibitions at the French pavilion were a significant entrenchment of the taste for Post-Impressionism, which was regarded not as an historical period, but as a body of art continuous with the main tradition of art in the 1920's. Degas and Jean-Louis Forain were shown in 1924, then Gauguin and Matisse, followed by Despiau, Toulouse-Lautrec, and Van Dongen; Zadkine and Monet were shown in 1932, Manet in 1934, then Degas again in 1936, and Renoir in 1938. The cumulative effect of these and related exhibitions is clear: French-based Post-Impressionism was now acceptable to the Italians, as well as to the French authorities.

In 1926, the last year in which Pica was Secretary General, complaints about the internationalism of the Biennale could be heard. Arturo Lancellotti collected his essays on all the Biennales since 1895 and complained of the recent invasion of "le nuove tendenze."[5] A later collection of essays, by Nino Barbantini, proposed the year 1932 as a symbolic time of choice: "Il labirinto e la Strada."[6] The road to follow was that of sincerity and "l'Italianità," and not the labyrinth of experimentation in which true human values are lost. Views like this are neither surprising nor very interesting when expressed by conservative writers on art. But it is remarkable that such views, expressed far more passionately, should originate within the Biennale itself. In 1930 the catalogue of the 17th Biennale carried a *Programma* signed by Pietro Orsi, President, Antonio Maraini, Secretary General, and Romolo Bazzoni. It takes as self-evident that Italian art in 1930 is no longer in need of education from foreign art. "The laws of cosmopolitanism derive especially from researches done in the convulsive and artificial ambience of Paris, where real talent is found together with willful artifice, voracious interests, and morbid ambition . . . The completely theoretical cerebralism of that cosmopolitan esthetic is particularly contrary to the spirit and sentiment of our [Italian] feelings." [7] The writers defend a "sensibile per l'Italia" as embodying "instinctive and healthy taste for the beauty dear to Raphael, for symmetry and proportion as laid down by Michelangelo, for expression and character as taught by Leonardo." [8] On one level this official statement is highly insulting to the participating countries; on another level, however, it is only a stronger formulation of the opinions of most of the foreign pavilions' organizers, including the French. The foreign art that was shown in Venice, when it was of recent date, tended to be the product of conservative modernism rather than of experiment. Thus, the Fascist view of art which is racial and retrospective can be paralleled with manifestations of "cosmopolitan" esthetics.

The belief that there are enduring canons of taste and that these had been set by three Italian artists of the early sixteenth century was obviously an attractive view to twentieth-century Italians (as well as to classicizing artists elsewhere, as we shall see). The belief would, of course, have been especially satisfactory to Italians, inasmuch as their recent art had not commanded much admiration. To chart the Italian roots of this nostalgic esthetic we can refer, first, to an exhibition at the Biennale of 1924 called *Sei Pittori del '900*. The painters (Anselmo Bucci, Leonardo Dudreville, Achille Funi, G. E. Malerba, Pietro Marussig, Mario Sironi) were members of the *Novecento Italiano* group, at whose exhibition in Milan the year before Mussolini had made a speech. The group is a hinge between a personally-based art on the one hand, and an official art on the other. Prior to the formation of this group, there had been the important *Valori Plastici* group, founded in 1918. It was pro-Italian and anti-Northern (and Northern, after all, in Italy means just about everybody else). However, its founders guaranteed its seriousness: they were Giorgio di Chirico, Alberto Savinio (di Chirico's brother, the poet), and Carlo Carrà. The group was an extension of another, *Pittura Metafisica,* which these three had formed in 1917. Ordinary objects and scenes, invested with serene grandeur and ominous calm, characterized Metaphysical Painting, as in di Chirico's still lifes, for example. It was an art of meditation, an art whose symbols encouraged us to infer the "soul" of the artist, a man who had withdrawn from the war and who rejected Futurism. The style quickly became not intro-spective, but nationalistic; not melancholy, but restrospective as a policy. By opposing "l'Italianità" (which is a compound of Italian feelings and a sense of nationality) to Impressionism, the Metaphysical Painters contrasted stillness to movement, the gravity of whole forms to the profusion of the fragmentary. This position, initially the outcome of personal necessity, was easily extendable to a classicizing and racist art theory, which is what happened.

The magazine *Valori Plastici* appeared in Rome in 1918, with an instant post-war, anti-transalpine esthetic. The "plastic values" of the movement's name meant a revival of the in-variant yet empathic solids of Giotto and Masaccio. Their forms were as self-contained as stones, but charged with human cor-respondences. Tranquil universals, derived from a noble past, were to preserve modern art from the dead-end of theory and the labyrinth of experimentation. Carrà's *Bathers* (fig. 28) shows the nostalgic figure style well; the forms are huge but reserved. The idea popularized by Bernard Berenson of tactile values linking the imagery of bodies with the spectator's body-image is implicit. Carrà wrote about Giotto in these highly personal terms: "The terrible plebeian beauty of this Tuscan wonder-worker, a beauty constructed on a few cardinal points, round which circles a sensitive arabesque."[9] The enduring type, rather than the specific case, is the aim of this and comparable works with simplified forms and interlocking compositions.

Let us consider, in very general terms, the overall stylistic character of the second phase of the Biennale compared to the first. Compared to the painterly Venetians and fluent Hungarians, compared to all the teasing, graceful, sensitized flow of the earlier painting, we are confronted with a prosaic, sober blandness (fig. 61). This is true of a remarkable amount of the new art of the 20's and 30's; there was a drive towards a closed surface and a soundly-designed rationalistic structure. In place of the vibrant or frivolous brushwork of late Salon painting, there is an anti-atmospheric continuity of surface. Forms are blocky, rounded, unbroken, not fragile, dimpled, or sketchy. Solid girls with thick ankles and no waists (fig. 74), posed in grave alternations of concave and convex form (fig. 62), parade through the classicizing figurative art of the period. Mediterranean hill-towns, streamlined nudes with no body-openings, reticent harlequins, these are elements of an emergent neo-classicism. Riccardo Schrotter's *Judgment of Paris* (fig. 29), as enacted by Mannerist robots, is the slick end of a spectrum which also contains Carrà's stony cast. Studio poses, with solid and planar model (fig. 79), replace the vivid, moist-lipped Society portrait as norm. Whereas an adaptation of Impressionism underlay the late art of the Salon, the simplifications of the Post-Impressionists are the origins of the new look (with Degas' contouring and Renoir's late plasticity retained from Impressionism). It is a placid amalgam of Masaccio, Cézanne, Modigliani, Matisse, and Picasso of the "classical" period.

The style of decoration in the Central Pavilion changed with the new taste. Gone are the overlaps of art and ornament, and of one art with another, that characterized the collaborative rooms of pre-war Biennales. Ornament is regarded as superfluous, or at least as something to be reduced to linear form, as in the cornice and archway surround of Gallery 29 in the Central Pavilion (fig. 26), seen here in 1928. The function of the gallery is now simply to display the works temporarily housed there in a residual classical framework. In fact, the flat wooden frames on the pictures introduce a lean touch of craft, as do the decorative three-legged chairs and octagonal table, a diminished echo of earlier abundance. In the more crowded Futurist gallery of this time (fig. 34), there is the same kind of boxlike space, defined by shriveled classical features, but here the space is divided by screens. The austerity of these rooms, not unlike the display principles still prevailing at the Biennale forty years later, is in accord with the flattened forms and simplified planes of the contemporaneous art. To compare the bare galleries of the 20's and 30's with a rare early example of simplicity of installation, the Gustav Klimt exhibition of 1910 (fig. 21), is instructive. The high elegance of this room is a unique decor that follows the style and the number of works being shown. The later austerity, on the contrary, is simply adaptive capacity; big and small works by one artist or many, in one medium or several, can be accommodated most easily in a space with minimal characterization.

This summarizing visual account can be supported by literary argument. One of the magic slogans of the first third of the twentieth century derives from a letter of Cézanne's, written in 1904 and published in 1907: ". . . to treat nature by the cone, the cylinder, the sphere; the whole placed in perspective, let each side of an object or a plane be directed toward a central point." [10] As a description of Cézanne's own practice the formula is absurd, particularly when the whole sentence is quoted to reveal his, of all people's, recommendation of central-vanishing-point perspective. He was presumably driven to write this by Emile Bernard's insistence that he verbalize his working methods. What he has put down here is, of course, only a first-year device of European art schools, but its banality is precisely what made it so serviceable to artists. It is certainly one of the supports of conservative modernism, the covert classicism of art between the wars.

Another dictum of the time, whose effect can be seen on many later artists, was that of Maurice Denis: "It must be remembered that a picture, before it is a picture of a war-horse, nude woman, or some anecdote, is essentially a plane surface covered by colors arranged in a certain order." [11] Denis also distinguished in a prophetic manner, between what he called "subjective deformation" in a painting (Van Gogh, for instance) and "objective deformation," by which he meant the art of Gauguin. [12] Denis links decorative flatness in art in the case of Gauguin with eternal laws of beauty and is thus able to reach the conclusion that Gauguin was "a kind of Poussin without classical culture." [13] This formula describes brilliantly the balance of traditional time-bound culture and modern decorative autonomy which underlies the bulk of conservative modern art in the Biennale's second phase.

Terms very similar to those of the 1930 *Programma* were used contemporaneously in Paris. Waldemar Georges, for example, in 1931 contrasted what he regarded as two antithetical ideas: "French School or Ecole de Paris." [14] "The international spirit of the School of Paris . . . is directed against the French School," which is, basically, the "spiritual and intellectual order [of] French classicism." [15] The School of Paris is "a handful of formulas" symptomatic of both "a collective neurosis" and "a fashion." [16] Georges offers a humanist's thumbnail sketch of the relation of Italy and France: "Italian art, according as it springs from Venice or from Tuscany, appeals to the senses or the mind. That pure melody and majestic *bel canto* of Italian poetry have been our [French] nurture from the cradle." [17] "But France outsails her" [18] in the seventeenth century. Thus Italian and French classicizing critics share a complementary and continuous culture; the torch may have passed from one to the other, but it is *one torch*. These quotations are from the magazine *Formes,* which condenses much of the opinion of conservative intellectuals on art between the wars. Georges was an admirer of the later di Chirico (whose gladiators he interpreted sympathetically) and of moderate artists such as Derain, whom he praised for escaping "the Scylla of Americanization and the Charybdis of negrophily—mankind as mere statistics and man as child of nature." [19] In 1931 the Royal Academy, London, held a large exhibition of French Art, and *Formes* responded

101

THE
BIENNALE
AND
FASCISM
1920-42

with a special number. Among many bouquets was W. G. Constable's nomination of France as "the chief repository of the humanist tradition," [20] after Italy, after Greece.

Classicism was professed by artists and writers with a classical culture and by those without it who nevertheless, like Gauguin, could be claimed as classical because of their belief in order. After the expressionistic and non-figurative art of the period before World War I, the post-war period became largely a time for the consolidation of earlier experiments or for the formulation of alternative doctrines. Hence, both within the canons of "modern" art and among the alternatives, a "return to order" was standard. One motive for the classical revival seems to have been a sense of lacking a center in our culture, missing a wholeness of identity such as that attributed to both the classical and Christian past. The return to order usually accompanied rejection of the twentieth century as shapeless, brutal, out of Grace. Classicism, in some form or other, was professed by almost every French intellectual between the wars. Cocteau, in his aptly titled book of 1923, *Un Rappel à l'Ordre,* wrote: "My journey to Greece was made at Montparnasse, later at Montrouge, and now in the rue la Boétie"; but the point is that he kept on making the classical trip. One member of the Action Française group, Robert Brasillach (best known as co-author of a book on the cinema), explicitly linked classicism with "Fascism, Italian and German," [21] and just before World War II argued for Corneille as a precursor of Fascism.[22] This is simply an extravagant statement of a general body of opinion. Nationalism and classicism could, after all, be convincingly linked in terms of the transmission of classical culture from ancient Rome to Renaissance Rome and thence to France. As for the peripheral countries not on this happy chain, it remained for their artists to possess as much of the grand tradition as possible, in whatever form they could.

The historical context of the classical revival of the 20's reveals, as a premise, the supremacy of Italian and French culture. Maurice Denis' hint became a book in Robert Rey's *La Renaissance du Sentiment Classique,* 1931, a study of Post-Impression-

ism as classicism's new form, a widely shared notion. Roberto
Longhi in 1927 had even treated Piero della Francesca as an
Umbrian Juan Gris, stressing to an unprecedented degree the elements of formal play in his art. Roger Fry published a study
of Cézanne in the same year which was based on his conviction
that Cézanne was nearer to Poussin than to modern artists.
Daniel-Henry Kahnweiler, dealer and critic of Cubism, applied
the idealizing and classicistic point of view to his painters and
found that it fitted one of them, Juan Gris, very comfortably.
All these writers, of course, are talking about possessing classicism from the inside, getting hold of an essential balance, a
strict elegance, without being distracted by the "trappings" of
real classical art.

The iconographic preferences of the regime and the requirements of the Sindicati delle Belle Arti, the Artists' Union, were
certainly reductions of art's absolute freedom in Italy. However, against this loss must be set the fact that many European
and American artists at this time were absorbed by an ideal of
monumentality in art, whose achievement meant creating a
viable public style. To do this on an individual basis was para-
doxical (as Léger discovered, for example), so some degree of
cooperation with national organizations was inevitable. Viewed
in terms of making a public art, the position of the Italian artist
is not to be compared with that of the contemporary German
artist who, under Nazism, was either subservient or persecuted.
The Italian artist had greater possibilities of adapting to the
pressures of his country, as they coincided with an artistic problem of topical interest. The desire for an epic style was not restricted to totalitarian countries. Closer parallels to programmed
Italian art than the art of Nazi Germany are revolutionary
Mexican murals and the murals produced in the United States
for the Federal Arts Project of the Works Progress Administration. Both north and south of the border, there was a passion
for public art, for the re-establishment of art in public spaces
by the presence of towering originals with legible subject matter. (Rivera, Siqueiros, and Orozco, are certainly the masters
of the style, with their control of colossal size and their unin-

103

THE
BIENNALE
AND
FASCISM
1920-42

hibited image-making coinciding with a social change that was affirmative in Mexico's history.)

Labor imagery is common to all the public art in this period of production difficulties; from harvesting the crops by hand, through assembly-line work, to tableaux of sorting the mail, public art stressed the theme of work. Production heroes—the worker, if male, the mother, if female—are universal. Where the styles of different countries diverge most startlingly is at the level of mythology. Mexican art is riven with reborn deities; German art is dominated by a narcissistic Nordic typology; the United States reveals a sentimental-historical fondness for Frontier folklore; and in Italy, classical references still occur, as in mosaics in the Palazzo Venezia, Rome, of Mussolini defending Europa from the (Communist) bull, and Mussolini as Triton embracing a sea-nymph. In general, however, Italy's official iconography of the period is Utopian and Imperialistic: the former is indicated by scenes inside the country of rich land and happy peasants; the latter celebrates force and war outside the country. Giovanni Barbisan's Umbrian revivalist *Our Best Friends Are the Peasants* (fig. 76), winner of a competition in 1936, is a clear example of the plentitude theme, and the Fascist Futurists specialized, as we shall see, in the marriage of Imperialism and Technology.

The character of official Italian art can be indicated for our purposes by easel paintings and portable sculptures in the Biennale, as well as by the subjects of competitions. During this period there were numerous prizes reflecting special interests of the state. In 1930 a prize for the best Maternity subject was initiated; other awards were for works dedicated to "the poetry of labor," inspired by "labor and industry," and inspired by agricultural activities, to make a partial list. These were offered, respectively, by the City of Venice, the General Fascist Confederation of Industry together with the Confederation of National Industrial Trade Unions, and the General Fascist Confederation of Farmers together with the National Confederation of Agricultural Trade Unions. 1930 is the year of massive state subsidy; there were more than twenty-five prizes from seventeen different official agencies or combinations of agencies. Other contributors were the National Fascist Party, the Rotary Club Italiano, the Adriatic Electricity Society, and the Industrial Port of Venice. None of the prizes were awarded to foreigners, and they remained a purely internal system of benefits. That the awards aroused national interest, or at least created public interest, can be seen from articles in such magazines as the Milanese *Sport Fascista,* which as early as August, within three months after the opening, faithfully discussed "Arte e Sport alle Biennale di Venezia." The splendid burst of prizes in 1930 subsided to awards from seven sources in the next Biennale and shrank still further subsequently, but, of course, prizes are not the only index of the desire for an epic, national art.

The Fascist Party prize in 1930 went to Arnoldo Carpanetti's *Incipit Novus Ordo* (fig. 69), a symbolic figure composition in which Mussolini is presented as a semi-military Hamlet. The black shirt, combined with the fact that Mussolini is the only still figure in an agitated picture, is responsible for this odd effect. Disordered crowd, orderly marchers, exhorting ghosts, all these elements surround the thoughtful hero. A favorite topic of Il Duce's artists was *The March on Rome,* derived from an event of 1924 when the scandal of the Giacomo Matteotti disappearance (later, murder) weakened Mussolini's position. A group of Blackshirts drove from Bologna to the edge of Rome and then marched, in an expression of confidence, to the dictator. As late as 1939 the march was still a subject for artists, figuring in a list of seven subjects in a competition open to all members of the Artists' Union who held permit 1939 XVII. (The other six subjects were: *Il Duce and the People, Squadronismo, Legionnaires, The New City, The Family,* and *The Empire.*)

1932 was the tenth year of the Fascist Era, and the Ministry of Corporations divided its prize for a commemorative painting among three artists. Gherardo Dottori's *Anno X* (fig. 71) is a montage of industrial and historic Italy, with a flight of planes swooping into the picture towards a ten-tiered, but obviously extendable, pyramid. A. P. Graziani's version (fig. 72) has a

105

THE
BIENNALE
AND
FASCISM
1920-42

phalanx of muscular Blackshirts marching through a simplified but radiant landscape (a kind of Froebelesque *quattrocento* style) into a gate marked X. Tommaso Cascella's *Anno X* (fig. 73) has an earth divided between muscle, on the left, and brain, on the right, with a reconciling central female figure who seems fecund enough to represent Charity. Heavenly support is also indicated by flying figures. Less formalized but no less symbolic is Manlio Giarrizzo's *Il Duce at Littoria* (fig. 75), a Fascist Party prize winner of 1934 (Littoria was land reclaimed under Mussolini's regime). The artist has set up a participative space by directing the attention of the waving, acclaiming, applauding, and watching figures out of the picture, to a point beside the spectator, as if that is where Il Duce stood. In this work, as in many allegorical pieces of the period, the forms are ranked one over another on a near-vertical picture plane. The reason for the flatness is not primarily decorative (though this is sometimes the effect), but the consequence of a desire to be explicit in all details of the communication. If Giuseppe Virgili's *Roman Civilization,* 1938 (fig. 37), for example, were spatially naturalistic, the expressive parallelism of the workers' poses would be unclear; the more naturalistically a work records a specific situation, the weaker its effect as paradigm.

The nude, which hovered ambiguously between neutral artistic theme and erotic subject in the early Biennales, continues to appear in the 20's, sometimes as convention and sometimes with a topical undercurrent. In 1930, the Patriarch of Venice forbade his clergy to visit the Biennale, and the Pope backed him with an attack on art "divergent from the spirit of Christian morality." This reaction was not prompted, as in 1895, by one objectionable item, but by an excess of nudes. In retrospect, however, the nudity of the period is less often voluptuous than biological and social in emphasis. The male nudes, whether adolescent or fully male, were uniformly fit, thus serving to support both the Fascist emphasis on athletics and the "demographic campaign." This was a plan whereby bachelors were taxed because of their unmarried status and prolific women rewarded. The female nudes, whether nubile or maternal, were iconographically apt to the campaign of procreation, as were the expectant or virile males. Here is a clear case of traditional iconography serving Fascism, though rather discreetly, while the Patriarch's and the Pope's artistic advisers had become alienated from both state policy and public interest. In this context, a moderate painting like Amerigo Canegrati's *Mother* (fig. 70), winner of the 1930 Maternity prize, takes on extra meaning; with the impassive face, the seated pose with crossed wrists and ankles, the figure becomes nothing less than a pregnant Modigliani.

Ardengo Soffici was one of the newer artists to be shown at the Biennale. Before the war, he had lived in Paris for seven years and was in a strong position, therefore, to expose the Biennale's one-sidedness. In 1909, in the Florentine magazine *La Voce*, he attacked the continued absence of the Post-Impressionists and of Picasso. When in 1926 Soffici was given a one-man show, he was surrounded, as we have seen, by just these artists, except for Picasso. In the meantime he had joined the Futurist movement in 1912 and left it in 1915. (In August 1910, incidentally, the Futurists had scattered leaflets from the Torre dell'Orologio attacking Venice's retrospective culture.)

In 1926 Futurism arrived irresistibly in Venice, though not with the original group, of course: Boccioni had been killed in the army and most of the others had adopted various forms of neo-classicism. (Gino Severini, for example, had published a book titled *Du Cubisme au Classicisme* in 1921). Fascist Futurism, as the new group should be called, retained connections with the original Futurists in the person of F. T. Marinetti. Owing to Marinetti, the Biennale was used to promote a group of artists antithetical to both the values of the first phase of the Biennale and to the style of all other Fascist-sponsored art. The presence of the new Futurists in the Giardini is one of the internal contradictions of the Biennale's second phase. The explanation is Marinetti's eminence in the Fascist Party (fig. 8) which earned him Mussolini's direct patronage. Their connection goes back more than ten years to the time they were both arrested for pro-war, pro-French demonstrations.

107

THE
BIENNALE
AND
FASCISM
1920-42

When Marinetti launched a Futurist magazine the first contribution to the first number was the following:

My dear Marinetti
I cordially approve your initiative in the constitution of a bank of credit especially for artists. I think that you will know how to surmount the obstacles of the usual misoneists. In any case, my letter will serve you as viaticum.

Ciao, with friendship.
Mussolini [23]

The Futurists (the original group which is meant when one refers to Futurism without any qualifying term) were five artists who stayed close to one another until at least 1914. In this year a clump of new artists was admitted to the First Free Futurist Exhibition in Rome. Two of the artists were destined, if that is the word, to become central to the second Futurism: Enrico Prampolini and Fortunato Depero. However, it must be understood that the key figure was not an artist at all, but Marinetti, poet, senator, and impresario with a driving power to attract or invent new talent and to create publicity. His remarkable ability to proselytize is shown by his endless supply of fresh artists. In 1926 the first Fascist Futurist show included Balla, Boccioni (a memorial gesture), and Russolo, and no fewer than twenty new artists. In 1928 he produced more Futurists and, finally, ten years later, the year before World War II, he was able to present a show of thirty artists called Futurists. Here, incidentally, can be seen the beginning of a characteristic psychology of post-war Italian artists, namely their receptivity to programs and to topical example. It is a new breed of adaptive artists, operating in ways quite different from the solid, normative style of the artists of the first phase of the Biennale.

Fascist Futurism represented an extrapolation of the machine-awareness of Futurism, but it was partially separated from specific objects. This meant that a greater degree of abstraction was possible than in earlier Futurism.[24] This less iconic imagery was represented by Marinetti and by Prampolini as lyrical and universalizing. They shared that vulgarization of esthetics in the twentieth century which identifies generality of representation with universality of content. As the details of machine forms were reduced, what took their place was supposed to be a spiritual evocation of energy, separated from the hardware that generated it. A kind of transcendence was implied, but at the same time, the works often were more prosaic than those that maintained exact references. The effect of Futurist painting in the 20's is less universal than operatic, less a fantasied world of liberated energy than an awkward Baroque revival. Marinetti, for example, called for the new Futurists to "enter into close contact with the world of clouds, fog, transparency, thickness, volume."[25] In doing so he is, probably unintentionally, insisting on a scenic continuity for Futurism, stressing a kind of space reminiscent of Pietro da Cortona or G. B. Tiepolo's decorative schemes.

The Biennale of 1932 included a Futurist section of what Marinetti called *aero pittori,* examples of which had been exhibited the year before in Rome at the Camerata degli Artisti. He wrote in the catalogue for Venice: "The changing perspectives of flight constitute an absolutely new reality which has nothing to do with the reality of traditional terrestrial perspective."[26] The celebration of an imagery of flight is essential to later Futurism in terms of the horizonless landscape, either as the earth viewed from above or as portraits of the sky. The first artist to tackle flight in terms of a new space is Kasimir Malevich, who related his abstract paintings to the vertical vision of the aviator or of people on the ground looking up at planes in flight. His theory was discussed in *Die Gegenstandslose Welt,* published by the Bauhäus in 1927. Malevich identified the early Futurist environment with trains, cars, ships, bridges, skyscrapers, dirigibles—reserving the free sensation of flight for his own Suprematist art. There can be little doubt that Marinetti's call for a more spiritualized art of the machine, as well as his invention of aero-painting, is an attempt to leapfrog over Malevich.[27] However, except for Prampolini's aerial paintings, *aero pittori* remains as bound to the concrete spectacle of hard-

109

THE
BIENNALE
AND
FASCISM
1920-42

ware as was classical Futurism. Wings, struts, nacelles, props, clutter the foregrounds of aero pittura. Tato's *Mechanical Splendor* (fig. 35), with a tilted view of an airfield seen through the blur of an airplane's prop, is characteristic in this respect. The painting has a vertiginous aspect, somewhat like a Baroque altarpiece, in its blurring of air and ground. Prampolini's *Inhabitant of the Stratosphere* (fig. 36) carries an abstracted reference to cloud imagery, but at the same time the suspended form, with a twisted linear flight-path pattern below, resembles an *Assumption of the Virgin,* with the Virgin's girdle snaking down to St. Thomas. Marinetti's demand for the translation of continuous and amorphous forms tended to encourage miraculous or Baroque effects.

The later Futurists, it might be noted here, were open to Christian themes in a way that seems thoroughly compatible with Fascist policy. In 1921 Mussolini had declared that the only valid universal idea radiated from the Pope, and in 1929 he signed the Lateran Pact which gave sovereignty to Vatican City. To Mussolini, Roman Catholicism was useful as a symbol of Rome's historic greatness, a symbol, moreover, whose modern representatives showed themselves to be conciliatory. In 1931 Marinetti and Fillia published a manifesto of Sacred Futurist Art in which they pointed out the suitability of aeropainters to symbolize the infinity of Heaven and its angelic inhabitants. Thus, one strategy by which Fascist Futurism spiritualized its forms was by equating the exaltation of flight with an ecstatic imagery characteristic of religious art since the Renaissance. This connection is not one that the Futurists would have welcomed openly, but the demonstrative and operatic quality of Fascist Futurism was compatible both with Italian religious art and with official Italian patronage.

In the 1938 Biennale Futurist art appeared under the title *Futuristi Aero-pittori d'Africa e Spagna* which was, of course, a direct link to Italy's invasion of Ethiopia in 1935 and participation in the Spanish Civil War in 1936. Fascist theory regarded expansion as an index of the vitality of the state. Hence, the African invasion was regarded as a part of Mussolini's historical destiny in establishing the Third Rome (Ancient and Renaissance Rome being the others). Establishment of a Mediterranean-African empire was the necessary first step. The Futurists, undoubtedly programmed by Marinetti, loyally accepted their role as the artists of Imperialism. Vittorio Mussolini, a pilot, the son of Il Duce (who himself took flying lessons at the end of World War I), achieved brief celebrity by his comparison of a bomb exploding among a group of Ethiopian horsemen to a budding rose. The image is pretty near to the rhetoric of Fascist Futurists, who could see flights in biplanes as a preparation for painting Heaven.

Marinetti, in the Biennale catalogue for 1938, wrote in his hectic prose of "aerial painting, sculpture, and music as daughters of Fascist aviation and of Italian Futurism." [28] The connection of Muse and Mars was not new to Futurism (a 1916 show in Paris had been called *First Futurist Exhibition of Plastic Art of the War*), but the fusion represented by Marinetti of esthetic and political authority was new. Aside from connections between technology and empire, there are other links between Futurism and Fascism. The hero, war, and labor imagery of official art was strongly present in the Futurist section of the Central Pavilion in 1930 (fig. 34). It was equally strong a few years earlier in Prampolini's *Mussolini: Plastic Synthesis,* 1926 (fig. 31), which combines a classic bust, a modern steel helmet, and Benito's jaw. The work is not fundamentally different from Adolfo Wildt's bust of Il Duce, 1924 (fig. 30), which is straight classic revival, except for the grossness of the forms. Both are laudatory effigies of the man in power, though one is by a Futurist and the other by a specialist in leader-portraiture. A connection even exists between Marinetti's 1938 text and the 1930 text signed by Orsi, Maraini, and Bazzoni. Marinetti codified the always nationalistic moods of Futurism in the coined word "esterofilia," which can be translated as "foreign mania." This is clearly affiliated to "cosmopolitan cerebralism" and, like it, designed to separate the "real" Italian spirit from outside distraction and to disguise any external obligation.

111

THE
BIENNALE
AND
FASCISM
1920-42

When the Biennale reopened in 1920 there were, in addition to the Central Pavilion, seven national pavilions, Belgium, Hungary, Great Britain, Germany, Sweden, France, and Russia, in the order of construction. Between 1922 and 1938 more pavilions were added, until by the end of the 30's the layout of the gardens was close to its present form. (Additional real estate was acquired in 1932 when pavilions were built on the other side of the Canal di Sant'Elena.) Spain built a pavilion in 1922, Czechoslovakia 1926, the United States 1930,[29] Denmark and Poland 1932, Austria and Greece 1934, Roumania and Yugoslavia 1938. In this year the German pavilion was restyled in a harsh neo-classic (the cubic classicism of the Third Reich); the U.S.S.R., however, let the folksy antiquarianism of its pavilion remain, either as expressive of the unchanging Russian character or out of economy. During this period of foreign building a minimum of prizes went to foreign artists. There were two Germans in the 20's (Max Liebermann and Richard Pietzsch); in the 30's there were Jan Sluytens (Dutch) in 1932, Dunoyer de Segonzac (French) and Herman Haller (Belgian) in 1934, and in 1938 Ignacio Zuloaga (Spanish) and Hermann Hubacher (Swiss) shared the Premio de Duce, awarded this year for the first time; Blair Hughes Stanton, an English engraver, was also honored in 1938. It is clear that the transfer of responsibility for foreign art from Italian hands to commissioners in various foreign countries, administering their pavilions, had a double effect. The structure confirmed the isolationism of Italian culture, but at the same time tolerated the existence of, as it were, national sub-cultures. The autonomous foreign pavilions were operated by committees which either had no grasp of their host's indifference to foreign art or were so preoccupied by provincial terms of reference, such as conferring prestige on local artists and styles, that they did not press for a more equitable relationship. Otherwise, why build and maintain pavilions for so little return?

Between Biennales, in 1935, the Central Pavilion was used for an exhibition of *Forty Years of the Biennale*. Despite a four-gallery homage to "l'arte straniera," the show must be regarded as basically a renewed presentation of all the *rétardataire* Venetians, with a nominally fraternal embrace for the Futurists. The sentiment of *l'Italianità* was, therefore, divisible into smaller units, such as Venice against other city-states, when an opportunity presented itself. By 1934 the Central Pavilion was entirely Italian or, one is tempted to say, local in its exhibitions. The responsibility of representing international values was left entirely to the commissioners of foreign pavilions.

A combination of local prejudice, acquiescence in the host country's esthetics, and limited resources reduced the effective exhibition of international styles. Belgium, whose exhibition record was excellent, had nobody left to show except the Surrealists, but failed to exhibit René Magritte and Paul Delvaux; the Dutch went to painful lengths to avoid showing Mondrian or any other *De Stijl* artists. Nor was there any sign of Paul Klee in the Swiss pavilion; and although Greece had put up a new pavilion, there were really no artists to go into it.

It cannot be said that there were significant contributions from either the United States or Britain. Both countries continued to do what the sophisticated commissioners of other countries had learned to avoid, namely, to make every exhibition a group show. This may have satisfied the pressures of democracy at home, but it resulted in a series of inconsequential exhibitions by artists who failed to interest Italians, let alone Europeans. In 1930 the American pavilion had a customarily diffuse exhibition, including Stuart Davis, Rockwell Kent, Edward Hopper, Augustus Vincent Tack (the Washington Augusto Giacometti), and Cecilia Beaux (who was, in 1911, the first woman on the jury of the Carnegie Institute's annual exhibition, later the Pittsburgh International). Meanwhile, in the British pavilion was a group consisting of Jacob Epstein, Henry Moore, John Skeaping (an animal carver), W. R. Sickert, Glyn Philpot R.A., and Sir William Rothenstein, a group to chill the most staunch anglophile of 1930. Probably the best press coverage the American pavilion received was in 1934 when it was nicknamed *Il Casa "Davies" alla Biennale* by the *Progresso*

113
THE
BIENNALE
AND
FASCISM
1920-42

Italo-Americano. A portrait of Marion Davies by a Polish artist turned up clandestinely in the pavilion, after Mrs. Juliana Force of the Whitney Museum had laid out the show. It was presumably put there on the initiative of William Randolph Hearst for the sake of the film star's reputation. Before the picture could be removed it was seen by the King Emperor of Italy, who remarked, "It's a beautiful portrait," and by the Crown Prince, who observed, "Pretty girl," according to the newspapers.

The early Biennales, for all their stylistic restriction, represented an international culture. When the Biennales of the second phase reveal a general style it was symptomatic rather than purposeful. The forms taken by the return to order, and by the stress on ideality, constitute an infra-structure of shared, but at the time not openly recognized, assumptions. As we saw, it had been characteristic of the Salon artists to reduce the rhetoric of the Grand Manner by crossing it with genre painting, and the genre elements were frequently sociological in implication. Subject matter, as a result, was removed from the simple hierarchic classifications of high and low, serious and comic. The Fascist artist, on the other hand, and the neo-classics in general, wanted to revive the image of the hero in the proportions of an epic art. The iconographic base for such an art (except for the descendants of Cézanne's and Renoir's late bathers, which are iconographically *déraciné*) had to be nationalistic, because an epic art requires themes common to the artist and his audience. There has yet to be an obscure public art.

A Royal Decree of January 13, 1930, signed by Vittorio Emanuele, confirmed a law of 1928, N.3229, regarding the Biennale (see p. 15) by which the Esposizione Biennale Internationale d'Arte was officially recognized as a permanent institution with supremacy over all Italian competitors. It is worth noting that this high-level authorization of the Biennale took place shortly before the publication of the nationalistic *Programma.* Another Royal Decree, July 21, 1938, N.1517, extended, but did not basically alter, the Biennale's responsibilities.[30] There is some additional bureaucratization, but it is interesting mainly for its official recognition of the Biennale's extended activities, beyond what was called, with especial appropriateness at this time, "arte figurativa."

In 1930 provision was made for exhibiting Venetian craft objects, a recrudescence of the pre-war decorative room schemes, but on the scale of objects for summer tourism. In the same year a Music Festival began, followed in 1932 by the annual, not biennial, International Film Festival. In 1934 a Theater Festival was started, but only the Film Festival, which is timed for later in the summer than the art exhibition, still prospers. The first Film Festival included *Mädchen in Uniform, Das Blaue Licht, A Nous la Liberté,* and, from the United States, *Bring 'Em Back Alive, Frankenstein,* and *Dr. Jekyll and Mr. Hyde* (the Rouben Mamoulian version). The expansion of the Biennale's activities into other arts was logical, given the continuing success of the biennial art exhibition, but, at the same time, a reminder of the increasing role of tourism in the economy of historical cities. In the nineteenth century the exhibition became a medium, with definite channel characteristics of its own; in the twentieth century, a city itself could become a medium, compounded of famous architecture, recurrent festivals, and tourist industries. Venice is itself a communicative pattern, a geo-temporal work of art.

The prize winners of the last three Biennales of the second phase bring political motives into the open. In 1938, while Mussolini was backing General Franco in Spain, the Grand Prize winner was a traditionalist Spaniard, Zuloaga; in his portrait of the bullfighter *Belmonte* (fig. 78), a carefully painted figure is set on a perfunctory background, in the sort of layered duplex that many academic artists affect, presumably to give extra plasticity and presence to their sitters. Bullfight imagery (Lorca's, Picasso's, Hemingway's) was much used by left-wing intellectuals, but Zuloaga's glittering rendering of a matador's suit is more like an aristocrat in fancy-dress and, hence, right-wing in its associations. Since the early days, the Hungarian pavilion had always been packed full of artists but had received little attention. Now Hungary was an ally of Italy, and in 1940

115

THE
BIENNALE
AND
FASCISM
1920-42

a Hungarian painter received first prize, for a rustic subject, a turgid evocation of brute strength in heavy flat patterns (fig. 80). In 1942 another Hungarian artist was honored (not since 1905 and 1907, when Ferenczy and Laszlo both won prizes, had Hungarian artists had it so good); Artur Kampf won the Grand Prize for an historicist painting, *The Offering of the People* (fig. 81). In a hastily converted room (note the silver on the table), all kinds of guns are being collected from people in all walks of life; the contrasted human types, however, are united in a common resolve. Here, in a nineteenth century whose problems are like those of today, as they say, the people are preparing to confront a common enemy. The work is a model of inspirational and patriotic topical history.

When war began in Europe in September 1939, preparations for the 1940 Biennale were naturally considerably advanced. The 22nd Biennale opened as planned, though without the participation of Austria, Britain, Denmark, France, Poland, and the U.S.S.R. However, the following countries were available to take part: Belgium, Germany, Holland, Hungary, Yugoslavia, Roumania, Spain, Sweden, Switzerland, and the United States. Exhibitions that had been planned in peacetime were not automatically cancelled, though no doubt the political situation was discussed at a high level. The presence of American art in the exhibition is a reminder of the general acceptability of Fascism, which has been referred to before. Attendance at this Biennale dropped, for the first time in its history, from six figures to five, to a mere 87,000. On the other hand, this number might be regarded by the French or the British, respectively occupied and blitzed by the Nazis in the summer of 1940, as extraordinarily high. (Incidentally, Italy entered the war in June, as the Biennale opened more or less, which showed that some of the high-level decisions had been a little off.) That Europe's communication system was able to move over three thousand art works and a substantial number of civilian visitors to an art exhibition, while half of Europe was fighting for survival, is as impressive as it is bizarre. In some respects the show went on much as usual. The third gallery of the Central

Pavilion showed the prize winners of the patriotic fresco competition announced in 1938, and elsewhere in the capacious building, Marinetti offered more aero-painting. In addition, there were *Simultaneous Aeroportraits,* as well as a survey of (non-simultaneous) Italian portraiture. The usual artists were present, from veteran Tito and quietist Arturo Tosi to Carrà and Achille Funi (both senior Novecento artists). Official portraiture increased: apart from the obligatory biennial busts of Il Duce and the King Emperor (in that order), there was sculpture of the Pope, Arnoldo Mussolini (Il Duce's brother), and Count Ciano (his son-in-law).

More remarkable than the 22nd Biennale, which was transitional between peace and war, was the 23rd in 1942, the first fully wartime Biennale, as was stressed at the time in the catalogue and in the Italian press. The British pavilion became the Army pavilion, the United States the Navy pavilion, and the French the Air Force pavilion. In addition to stirring official portraits and heroic effigies, there were occasional stylized scenes of combat, and documentary views of hospitals, submarine bases, seaplanes, infantry in the rain, and so on. This kind of imagery has a parallel, incidentally, on the other side, in paintings and drawings produced for the War Artists' Commission in England. The official artists' work was shown in an otherwise evacuated National Gallery. (Prampolini's influence was visible, oddly, in the Battle of Britain skyscapes of Paul Nash, with vapor paths and odd-shaped clouds.) At Venice, life went on, sometimes imperturbably, as with Gregorio Sciltian's portrait of *Il Conte Luigi Visconti di Modrone as a Jockey.* There was also a good sample of dancers, Olympias, Susannas, Aphrodites, and a *Giovanetta in piedi:* art taking care of the great cultural continuities at a time of crisis?

Antonio Maraini's introduction to the 1942 catalogue is a remarkable document. He laments that artists are short of materials, labor is expensive, transportation is hard to get, but the difficulties were surmounted, triumphantly, by people motivated by "Patria." "While the enemy reveals his incapacity to obey the duty to preserve the universal wealth of civilization, de-

117

THE
BIENNALE
AND
FASCISM
1920-42

stroying everything he can—undefended old towns, famous
for their monuments—Italy is reaffirming her mission of civilization, asking the nations of a new Europe—nations already
proving themselves victorious on the field of battle—to meet
for this austere rite of contemporary art." [31] Appropriately,
Joseph Goebbels, the Nazi Minister of Propaganda, attended
the rite, and he would, presumably, have confirmed the usefulness as propaganda for internal morale of the Italians' pro-
prietary sense of culture. This sense of cultural identity, which
nourished the best Italian painting after World War I, could
also be coarsened to aggressive nationalism, as in the *Programma* of 1930. The crudity of that text compares closely
to the 1942 Introduction; perhaps Maraini, the Secretary General under whom the Biennale became a Fascist instrument,
was the main author of the earlier jointly-signed piece. Goebbels' visit stressed the fact that this Biennale was essentially an
"Italo-Germanica Association." [32] Attendance now was down
to 76,000, but the ideological value of holding such an exhibition, after two years of war, was considerable. It affirmed the
Rome-Berlin axis, emphasized Italy's European role as "keeper
of the flame," and implied an illusory high level of stability and
leisure in the middle of war.

1. Helen Gerard, "The XVII Venice Biennale," *The American Magazine of Art,* XXI, No. 7 (1930).
2. Theodor Eschenburg, "The Breakdown of Democratic Systems between the Two World Wars," in *The Path to Dictatorship 1918-1933* (New York, 1966).
3. Expressionists at the Biennale included Van Gogh in the Dutch pavilion in 1926, the second School of Laethem St. Martin (Gustave de Smet, Permeke, Frits van den Berghe, Gustave van de Woestyne) in the Belgian pavilion in the same year, and Emil Nolde in the German pavilion in 1928. Such shows are significant as part of the few "modern" exhibitions to dissent from the prevailing School of Paris orientation.
4. Alessandro Stella, *Chronistia della Esposizione Internazionale d'Arte della Città di Venezia, 1895-1912* (Venice, n.d. [*ca.* 1912]).
5. Arturo Lancellotti, *Le Biennali Veneziane del Dopo Guerra* (Venice, 1926).
6. Nino Barbantini, *Biennali* (Venice, 1945).
7. *Programma,* Catalogue, XVII Biennale, 1930.
8. *Ibid.*
9. Quoted in Werner Haftmann, *Painting in the Twentieth Century.* (New York, 1965). (See "Towards a Comprehensive Style. Arts Between the Wars" for a synoptic account of the conservativism of the 20's and 30's.)
10. Paul Cézanne, *Correspondence,* ed. by John Rewald (London, 1941).
11. It is important to stress that this is the opening sentence of Maurice Denis' "Definition de neo-traditionnisme," first published 1890, reprinted in his *Théories 1890-1910,* (Paris, 1920 [2nd ed.]). Thus it was as obviously available as Cézanne's cone-cylinder-sphere cliché.
12. Maurice Denis, "De Gauguin et de Van Gogh au Classicisme," *loc. cit.*
13. Maurice Denis, "L'Influence de Paul Gauguin," *loc. cit.*
14. Waldemar Georges, "French School or Ecole de Paris, I," *Formes* (English ed.), No. 16 (June, 1931).
15. *Ibid.*
16. *Ibid.*
17. Waldemar Georges, "French School or Ecole de Paris, II," *Formes* (English ed.), No. 17 (September, 1931).
18. *Ibid.*
19. Waldemar Georges, "Derain's Message," *Formes* (English ed.), No. 19 (November, 1931).
20. *Formes,* No. 20 (December, 1931). This special number on French

119

THE
BIENNALE
AND
FASCISM
1920-42

art at the Royal Academy included Roger Fry's "Reflections on French Art," in which he declared: "France has formulated the true ethical code of the artist [out of] a heroic detachment from personal motives." Here, in the cult of impersonality, is another facet of the pseudo-classical opinion of the time.

21. René Wellek. "French Classical Criticism in the 20th Century," *Yale French Studies.* 38 (New Haven, Connecticut, 1967).

22. *Ibid.*

23. *Rivista d' Arte Futurista,* 1923. (Misoneists: a political party sworn to reunite Italy.)

24. The spatial aims of later Futurists, such as the spatial experiences of technology, but without the visible hardware, were not realized before Lucio Fontana's *Concetti Spaziali.* Though Fontana's Spazialismo became a movement in Milan it can only be usefully considered as a personal manifestation of Fontana's.

25. *Gazzetta del Popolo,* 1931, quoted by Rosa Trillo Clough in *Futurism* (New York, 1961).

26. Catalogue, XXI Biennale, 1938.

27. Incidentally, the first Manifesto of *Aeropittori* is of 1929, two years after the publication of Malevich's book. The time-lag seems just right. The signatories were: Balla, Marinetti, Prampolini, Depero, Gherardo Dottori, Fillia, Benedetta, Somenzi, and Tato.

28. Catalogue, XXI, Biennale, 1938.

29. Incidentally, there are various ways to finance a pavilion, if the government fails to do so; the Danish pavilion was funded by the Foundation Ny-Carlsberg and the American pavilion by the Grand Central Galleries, New York, a dealer in old masters. Both gestures of good will, rescuing the art of each country from the cauldron of the Central Pavilion, earned considerable prestige for the donors.

30. Romolo Bazzoni, *60 Anni della Biennale di Venezia.* See "I Regolamenti e la leggi."

31. Antonio Maraini, introduction to catalogue, XXII Biennale, 1942.

32. *Il Gazzettino* (Venice), September 1, 1942.

FIVE

ART
AND THE
EXPANDING
AUDIENCE

The instability of taste has become apparent since the eighteenth century, the time at which the existence of antithetical esthetic doctrines and taste cultures came into the open. Passionate differences existed earlier among artists and their supporters, such as the dispute of the *Rubenistes* and *Poussinistes,* but both sides debated, in the last analysis, within an agreed-on definition of art. By the eighteenth century, along with the development of the novel and the expansion of theater audiences, the rise of public art exhibitions and increased print distribution introduced truly divisive factors. The small cultivated public for art, as it existed in every country, supported a uniform idealistic view of art; it was now faced by a quantitatively powerful alternative. What might have happened is that the separate cultures would have acquired different vocabularies, just as they developed different functions. As this did not occur, the supporters of elite culture tried to get esthetic control over the diffusion and popularization of the arts by means of an existing vocabulary and on behalf of their own taste culture.

Fine art, as traditionally defined in terms of elite satisfaction, was set in a position of antagonism to popular culture and its consumers. "The highest effort of genius, in every work of art," wrote William Hazlitt, "can never be understood by the generality of mankind." [1] "The greater the number of judges, the less capable must they be of judging . . . thus the decay of arts may be said to be the necessary consequence of its progress." [2] Thus, by the second decade of the nineteenth century, when Hazlitt wrote, there existed not only a rift between fine art and popular culture, but also a theory aimed to disenfranchise the big audience entirely. Beauty and seriousness were allocated to the small group; banality and sensationalism were attributed to the larger group. Beauty traditionally possessed an intellectual content which could not be available to the untrained audience. Popular culture, viewed as entertainment, was supposed to encourage audience passivity, whereas art was demanding. Matthew Arnold defined the aim of culture as being "to draw ever nearer to a sense of what is indeed beautiful, graceful, and becoming, and to get the raw person to like that." [3] As to this raw person, let us consider T. S. Eliot's definition of him in quantity: "We see generation after generation of untrained readers being taken in by the sham and the adulterate in their own time—indeed preferring them, for they are more easily assimilable than the genuine article." [4] These quotations from Hazlitt, Arnold, and Eliot concur in their image of the public as an appetitive beast, totally unqualified for esthetic judgment. Such views are typical and could be extended tediously. The question must be raised, however, as to what extent an elite definition of culture can be absolute in a period of increased education and cultural diversification.

Clement Greenberg, when he considered this problem, allowed for the relativity of values, then wrote: "Yet there does seem to have been more or less of a general agreement among the cultivated of mankind over the ages as to what is good art and what bad. Taste has varied, but not beyond certain limits." [5] Henry Geldzahler has recorded how "unpleasant" was his "realization that the *true* audience for new art is so small and so specialized." [6] He finds *"true* understanding rare." [7] It is one thing for Hazlitt, at an earlier stage of the tension between elite and mass audiences, to dismiss "mankind," but it is something else, at the center of a period of mass consumption of art, to repeat the argument and let it rest on what is meant by "true." To return to Greenberg, let us see what he, as a representative of "the cultivated of mankind," feels at a big exhibition. "At the Biennale in Venice in 1954, I saw how de Kooning's exhibition put to shame not only the neighboring one of Ben Shahn, but that of every other painter his age or

123

ART
AND
THE
EXPANDING
AUDIENCE

under in the other pavilions." [8] The record of experience is sufficient to blot out every artist but one; it is no doubt true, in terms of an individual variable, but in the absence of argument it is not very interesting. Meanwhile, in another part of the Giardini, there was Douglas Cooper: "Beside Munch, the later expressionistic painters exhibiting—for example, de Kooning (U.S.A.), Appel (Holland), or F. Bacon (Great Britain)—appeared shallow, boisterous, and uncertain." [9]

If we are to discuss the new audience, which is in part the audience for such institutions as the Biennale, we need to be able to refer to large groups objectively. George Rudé [10] has distinguished between at least four types of crowd, summarized thus: (1) the audience-crowd, which attends theaters, lectures, games, bullfights and art exhibitions; (2) active crowds, like the groups participating in Mardi Gras or Carnival or in student demonstrations; (3) escape or panic crowds, as in the case of runs on banks or flights from fire; and (4) the aggressive crowd, typically involved in a strike or a riot. Writers on art and culture continually blur these distinctions, owing to a prejudice against the "fickle masses" and the "insensate mob." The language of elite art, which is shaped for certain situations, is thus imposed on other phenomena that it does not fit. The result is that the audience-crowd at the Biennale inappropriately acquires some of the impulsive, instinctive, destructive qualities of other crowd-types.

When we speak of the expanded audience for art, there is a tendency to relate it exclusively to mass media, especially in the last twenty years. So far as art is concerned, we can see the communications increase in full operation in the nineteenth century. This is the period, as we discussed, of increased public exhibitions, as well as the conversion of royal art collections into the public domain. It is, also, a period of improved mails; compare, say, the meagre correspondence of Sir Joshua Reynolds in the eighteenth century with the copious letters of Vincent van Gogh and the increase in the capacity of the channel becomes evident. Freedom to move among countries, at greater speed and in safety, as well as the emergence of magazines, amplified the amount and accuracy of information about art, as, indeed, about everything else. In discussing the history of the Biennale it must be kept in mind that we are continually dealing with participants in a radically reformed communications system. Both the artists and the audience were involved, and we are today their heirs, in an intensified but otherwise similar situation. Exhibitions and reproductions have in common the fact that both are channels that move the work of art, or its image, out of its original context of creation or ownership into a public situation. There are fears that distribution and duplication in some way corrode the value and presence of originals. Edgar Wind has argued that "the medium of diffusion tends to take precedence over the direct experience of the object, and more often than not the object is conceived with this purpose in view. We are given the shadow for the thing." [11] Harold Rosenberg argues similarly that "the art in an art book is a collection of substitute images," [12] and that "global distribution makes art images available everywhere, but shorn of the experiential synthesis represented by the originals." [13] This is oddly reminiscent of Socrates defending oral communication against the phonetic alphabet which will "create forgetfulness" and give "not truth, but only the semblance of truth." [14] What is interesting is that these two writers, the speculative iconographer and the ex-Marxist essayist, one in Oxford and one in New York, are both so sensitive to the autonomy of art. We can summarize their position, perhaps, as: artistic autonomy versus public information. Both writers seem to believe in a kind of communication overkill brought on by exhibitions and reproductions. However, there is no evidence that exposure and multiplication degrade original works of art. Both exhibitions and reproductions move works of art, or their surrogates, into new relationships, but this seems to me entirely within the legitimate usage of an art that is mobile.

Are we not, as a result of the collision of ideas about art as autonomous and art as public information, in the presence of an imaginary problem when we speculate on the damage done to a work of art by familiarity? It is true that one sophisticated

125

ART
AND
THE
EXPANDING
AUDIENCE

group may withdraw its interest from the work of an artist or period appropriated by another and larger taste culture. However, such works of art are not historically soiled by adventures in the history of taste. Marcel Duchamp has not, after all, destroyed the Mona Lisa. Nor does it seem to reflect a real problem to say that mass art puts elite art under pressure. Both kinds of art are produced by different people for different occasions (though, possibly, for the same complex consumer). When an elite artist receives some of the lustre of mass media fame, there is no built-in degenerative mechanism, either in his psyche, or in his art.

Evidence of the change in the size of the audience for art is to be found everywhere, including the sale of mass produced postcards and of reproductions. Fernand Khnopff has recorded a connection of printing-technology and the painting of a fellow-artist. "When pictorial postal cards became the fashion in Belgium, Mr. Dietrich, the publisher, of Brussels, was not slow to suggest to Cassiers that he should execute a series . . . which were quickly succeeded by the facsimiles of the water-colors known as the *Big Mill, Evening Effect, View of Dordrecht, The Four Windmills.*" [15] The art world was sufficiently large at the end of the nineteenth century to support crowds of Salon artists, in their various styles, a large number of avant-garde artists with their own international taste culture, and a mounting industry of reproductions. This is a diverse and professional art world, developed beyond unification by any aristocratization of taste. Probably the best image for conceiving the situation is that of a continuum, in which different arts co-exist and in which changing connections can occur. This seems a more appropriate image for an abundant and mobile period of art than the rigid taste-pyramids with which the history of taste is littered.

A speed-up in communications coincided with the expansion of the size of the audience. The process can be seen if we consider the diffusion of three art movements: Impressionism, Neo-Impressionism, and Futurism, covering the period from 1874 to 1914. The hostility to the Impressionists in the 1870's is overfamiliar, while the degree of acceptance they received on an international scale in the 1890's, in particular Monet, is underemphasized. Knowledge of Neo-Impressionism was more rapidly circulated, first from Georges Seurat to other French artists in 1886; then to a strong Belgian group by 1889. Marinetti's "Foundation Manifesto of Futurism" is of 1909, and the "Technical Manifesto of Futurist Painting" 1910; then, between February and October, 1912, there were Futurist exhibitions in Paris, London, Berlin, Brussels, The Hague, Amsterdam, and Munich. As early as 1911 Apollinaire wrote on the new group in *The New York Sun*. Though secession is always available to those artists who want it, and to some who don't, in the years before World War I a well-functioning communications network clearly existed which reduced to virtual immediacy the once protracted time-lag between artist and artist, and artist and audience.

Art critics are now faced with the linked problems of (a) unprecedented quantity (of works and artists) and (b) multiplicity (of possible styles). Their subject has become uncontrollable; its boundaries are no longer clear and its scale is no longer compact. This holds true, also, for the art of the past, which obviously is steadily increasing as a result of the passage of time, and of ever-more-sophisticated techniques of inquiry into past periods. The global scale of knowledge has weakened the authority of the individual critic, who will be unknown or misinterpreted beyond the effective diameter of his ideas. In fact, the audience is far larger than formerly, but consensus is harder to obtain as a result. A network of information and opinion has replaced the drive for uniform validated standards which motivated earlier critics.

As the usage of art is increased by stepped-up distribution, there is a corresponding increase in the variables of experiencing art. The more widely a work of art is seen, the more divergent become its readings. The uniqueness of the spectator's experience is certainly not reduced by the extended communications network. On the contrary, first-person awareness is more singular than ever, as art is encountered in changing contexts. The

127
ART
AND
THE
EXPANDING
AUDIENCE

lowering of taste and standardization of values, alleged to be the crowd's contribution to modern art, are thus the fictions of elite-oriented critics. Anybody who has seen the work of artists of one country under the influence of artists of another is usually more aware of change than conformity. The global scale of art today weakens the consensual effect of national groups of critics anxious to define their own country's art as normative. Magazines, exhibitions, and travel all tend to modify standard responses to art by increasing the variable information available to different individuals in the same field. If it is agreed that there are no uniform responses to the same symbolic stimuli, it can be seen that standardization is not likely to be the esthetic result of large exhibitions. In fact, we have a spectator situation analogous to that which Historicism conferred on nineteenth-century artists and architects in freeing the study of each period style of irrelevant value systems. For the spectator, it means that the reality of his personal response need not be relegated to ignorance or, at best, innocence, compared to the authority of art criticism.[16] The spectator's freedom of interpretation is a function of his responsibility for his own reactions, like his own walking pattern in a large exhibition. Such a show tends to be staged somewhat scenically, but unlike the theater there is no clear division of the space into stage (spectacle) and auditorium (spectators). On the contrary, exhibition space is continuous and multi-directional, even in an axial suite of rooms; sequential displays are not inviolate routes. The spectator's capacity to move resembles the freedom of a visitor in picturesque gardens; movement there was from moment-to-moment, with surprises of scale and content built into the landscaping. A big exhibition is more like such a garden than it is like a theater, because the spectator is actively precipitated among unexpected works rather than being the occupant of a fixed zone, as in the theater.

The oldest regular exhibition of contemporary painting after the Biennale is the exhibition at Pittsburgh, first called the *Annual Exhibition* and from 1920 the *International.* It started in 1896, under the direct sponsorship of Andrew Carnegie, whose idea it was that "American art, if placed side by side with the best European art, would be stimulated to achieve qualities of its own and not imitate works from abroad." [17] Here is an echo of the educative optimism of the early Biennale. During the 1920's, the School of Paris was well represented; in 1927 Matisse took first prize and in 1930 Picasso. The annual Pittsburgh shows contributed to the general build-up of knowledge in the United States about modern art, then associated with Europe, but no specific benefits seem traceable to the institution. Neither paternalistic largesse nor civic organization seemed able to affect the production of new art in either America or Italy. The development of American art was not influenced by the shows; assimilation and transcendence of European art had to wait for a later occasion. (Such resistance by artists to what is expected of them is, incidentally, a reason for thinking that the accelerated rate of communications in art is not, in fact, likely to rush art to a series of fashionable climaxes.)

A few statistics make clear that the public interest in art was not restricted to Venice: in 1907, a record year for Pittsburgh owing to the opening of new galleries, attendance was more than 142,000.[18] This is considerably below the Biennale's 357,000 for the same year, but it is a high figure for a city that is neither a capital nor a monument. In 1931, attendance was 161,747, compared to the Biennale's 1930 attendance figure of 193,000.

In the first year of the Pittsburgh exhibition, John Lavery and Jean François Raffaeli (both well respected at Venice) took the first two medals for Europe, but the other three prize winners were American (Cecilia Beaux, Winslow Homer, and Frank W. Benson). This ratio was repeated in 1897, but gradually the number of winning Americans increased, until in 1901 the first three prizes went to Americans: Alfred H. Maurer, Ellen W. Ahrens, and Edmund C. Tarbell. In 1903 all five winners were American, a faithful echo of the constitution of the juries which were either mainly or totally American. Here is the equivalent of the chauvinism so often

129

ART
AND
THE
EXPANDING
AUDIENCE

demonstrated by Italian jurors in Venice, happily confident of their friends' and countrymen's greatness. The conferring of prizes on American artists in a big-scale show was the factor most likely, in the long run, to foster the native independence that Carnegie wanted.

In 1907 the first prize in Pittsburgh went to a French painter with a flashy, painterly style, for which he was well named, Gaston La Touche, and the second prize went to Thomas Eakins. It is easy enough in retrospect to know that the jury was wrong about La Touche, seen frequently at Venice, and especially wrong about his merits compared to Eakins'. It is equally easy to complain of the absence of, say, Fauvism from the 1907 show, let alone the absence of Fauves among the prize winners. The present (call it 1907), while it is being lived, is dense and complex; the form that we confer on it later is highly arbitrary. What we need when approaching the history of nineteenth- and twentieth-century art are techniques that are not destructive of the unparalleled stylistic diversity of the periods. Late Salon artists or provincial American painters should not be sacrificed to an esthetic more homogeneous than the art it has to describe. We need to develop a sense of the different taste cultures and their respective esthetic standards rather than to codify our own preferences. Simply to reverse the 1907 jury's decision about La Touche and Eakins is not the way to understand the period, or either artist.

The emphasis that we place on originality, either of idea or unique handling, has blocked recognition of other possibilities in art. For instance, we recoil from the banal in art; clichés have been signals for the withdrawal of serious attention. However, clichés can function as summarizing images—of the life of an artist with a set subject, or of a period style, or of a national character. Stereotypes condense out of period forms and iconographical themes. When this happens it is the repetition, at least as much as the variation, which is communicative; it is the sameness more than the new twist which is relevant. Clichés in art are shaped by collective and sometimes anonymous tradition as well as by personal authorship. Van Gogh, for example, was an admirer of popular culture for its impersonal and accessible imagery. Among subjects that he listed as admiring in illustrated magazines are *The Foundling, The Girl I Left Behind Me, Waning of the Honeymoon, Sunday Evening at Sea,* and *Cabin of Emigrants' Ship.*[19] The cliché is impersonal as an invention, a form of common property, and it is immediately engaging. The titles listed by Van Gogh nearly ninety years ago are still legible. Clichés are supposed to lose their impact through overuse, but stereotyped images such as these have an obstinately long life. Historical distance can, in fact, reveal freshly the stereotypes of preceding periods, not by converting them to an individualistic form of art, but by clarifying their public shape. La Touche's painting (fig. 52), for instance, with nymphs leaning intimately on a dying faun, if viewed as a cliché of Arcadian eroticism rather than as exploration, has its status and purpose in a diversified art world.

131
ART
AND
THE
EXPANDING
AUDIENCE

1. William Hazlitt, quoted in Leo Lowenthal, *Literature, Popular Culture, and Society* (Englewood Cliffs, New Jersey, 1961).

2. *Ibid.*

3. Matthew Arnold, *Culture and Anarchy* (London, 1869).

4. T. S. Eliot, *The Use of Poetry and the Use of Criticism* (London, 1933).

5. Clement Greenberg, *Art and Culture* (Boston, 1961).

6. Henry Geldzahler, "The Art Audience and the Critic," *Hudson Review*, XVIII (January, 1965).

7. *Ibid.*

8. Greenberg, *Op. Cit.*

9. Douglas Cooper, "Reflections on the Venice Biennale," *The Burlington Magazine*, XCVI, No. 619 (1954).

10. George Rudé, *The Crowd in History* (New York, 1964).

11. Edgar Wind, *Art and Anarchy* (London, 1958).

12. Harold Rosenberg, *The Anxious Object* (New York, 1964).

13. *Ibid.*

14. Plato, *Phaedrus,* trans. by W. C. Helmbold (New York, 1956).

15. Fernand Khnopff, "A Belgian Painter: M. Henri Cassiers," *Studio,* XXVI, No. 3 (1902).

16. There is a tendency to view the reactions of art critics to works of art as signs of the real meaning and hence as more true than lay reactions. In fact, art criticism is not a model for the personal experience of each spectator. Art criticism is concerned with meaning at a social and academic level as sharable commentary. As such it does not pre-empt other readings; it co-exists with them.

17. Department of Fine Arts, Carnegie Institute. *Retrospective Exhibition of Paintings from Previous Internationals,* Introduction by Leon Anthony Arkus (Pittsburgh, 1958).

18. *Ibid.*

19. Vincent Van Gogh. *Letters to Anton Ridder van Rappard* (London, 1936).

SIX

THE
AVANT-GARDE
IN A
GOLDFISH BOWL
1948-68

The wartime Biennale of 1942 was a logical culmination of the political functions assigned to art in the Fascist state; however, as open propaganda against the countries who, in 1945, "liberated" Italy, it could not be resumed in its old form. The institution was thoroughly devalued by its Fascist connections, and in any case, the imperialistic overtones of the 30's were clearly inappropriate to a defeated country. The new Special Commissioner (the title was formerly President) of the Biennale was Giovanni Ponti, who had been designated Syndic of Venice by the Veneto branch of the Committee of National Liberation. The new Secretary General, Rodolfo Palluchini[1] was an art historian, though not a specialist in the twentieth century. In the catalogue of the first post-war exhibition, Palluchini links the Biennale to "the new climate of liberty"[2] and reaffirms, as he says, the original educative aims and open policy of the Biennale. This is not exactly what happened in the early Biennales, but Ponti's and Palluchini's need was to go around Fascism to an immaculate origin. In fact, the Biennale, under Palluchini's guidance, did combine his art historian's respect for truth with the correction of injustice. For the first time the Venice Biennale presented a series of art historical exhibitions.

Before the post-war cycle of exhibitions could start, however, there were problems in the Giardini. Discussions on the resumption of the exhibition began in 1946, but the pavilions had to be restored before it was possible to act. During the war two film companies had used the pavilions, which were mostly rather summary in construction, at first for storage, and then towards the end of the war when Northern Italy was safer than

Rome, as studios for film production. Giovanni Battista Dell'Armi was, briefly, the first Special Commissioner; his assignment was the difficult administrative one of getting funds out of the post-war Government. The Ministro della Cultura Popolare and the Ministro dei Lavori Pubblici, as well as the film companies, paid compensation to the Biennale. Three years after the end of the war the 24th exhibition opened.

The exhibitions in homage to early modern artists and movements sometimes seemed to have the form of reparations, as with a French Impressionist exhibition in the German pavilion. The historicist impulse, however, reached beyond such ironies, and to appreciate the reasons for this we need to recall the state of modern art studies in the 40's. With a few exceptions the literature either emanated from the artists' friends or was written at a high level of abstraction, like the classicizing criticism of the 30's. There was an extraordinary shortage of objective information and an almost complete absence of material on non-French styles. Most of the useful literary sources to which we would automatically refer today were unavailable because of the war, or yet to be published. The organizers of the post-war Biennales set out to remedy this situation; a representative art history and the spirit of liberty concurred.

In 1948, as well as the Impressionist exhibition (which included Post-Impressionists, too), proposed by the art historian Roberto Longhi, there was a show of Metaphysical Painting (Carrà, di Chirico, Morandi). These artists are familiar now, but their early work was not accessible then. Other artists appeared in the Biennale, many of whom had been overlooked but now began to join the history of twentieth-century art. Austria showed Egon Schiele and Kokoschka; France showed Braque, Chagall, Picasso, and Rouault; Great Britain showed Henry Moore; and Paul Klee was exhibited at last, but by the Italians, not the Swiss. It cannot be stressed enough that the opportunity to see work by major artists of the century, to compare work from different periods of individual artists and to compare the artists with each other, had not been possible before. For the most part it was not until the later 40's that the

135

THE
AVANT-GARDE
IN
A
GOLDFISH
BOWL
1948-68

study of living (or recently dead) artists was conducted on any scale and with any thoroughness. (The previous unit of information had been the one-man show, rather than large comparative displays.) The change of purpose and the expansion of scale are important because they mark the definition of modern art in terms of art history; art history, instead of being a method for dealing with a past clearly separated from the present, now included recent, and sometimes new, art. The past and modern art became historically continuous.[3]

Modern art history was conspicuous at the Biennale of 1950.[4] Here were exhibitions of *Les Fauves,* Cubism, Futurism (the signatories of the *First* Futurist Manifesto only), *der Blaue Reiter* (or *Cavaliere Azzurro*), Flemish Expressionism, and various individuals, including Max Beckmann, Medardo Rosso, and le Douanier Rousseau. The School of Paris was amply represented, but so was non-French art; this was a corrective to the one-sided view of the century that had prevailed before the war. The German and Italian movements emerged from their marginal status, not in terms of a cultural ghost of the Axis, but as a legitimate re-evaluation. The justice of their reappearance can be seen by the fact that it has not been reversed, or doubted, since.

The Biennale's interest in art history led to its being sued by an artist. Giorgio di Chirico brought action against the Agency for showing a group of his early Metaphysical Paintings against his wishes. No invitation had been issued to him as the artist, and collectors had been approached without his consent. In 1951 the Court awarded di Chirico 250,000 lire and expenses, but the Court of Appeals reversed the judgment: owners' rights were upheld. The Court declared that the owners of works of art had the right to exhibit their property, unless prior arrangements had been made with the artist. Di Chirico's early work has had avant-garde esteem for years and his later work has had popular Italian acclaim; the two periods of his work have been accepted, that is to say, by two different taste cultures. Hence the spectacle of a man opposed to his own early work. (Given the dichotomy of modern and academic art, nobody has ever tried to take a unified view of di Chirico's complex development.) In 1956, incidentally, when his work was shown again at the Biennale, this time with his agreement to judge from the catalogue text, written by Isabelle Far, no dates were given for the paintings.

The majority of the historically-oriented exhibitions in the post-war Biennales have not been definitive or even, at times, adequately prepared, but there are reasons for this. The Biennale is under-financed, and also it is a spectacle, in the tradition of nineteenth-century spectacular shows. The importance of these post-war shows lies not in their perpetuation in commendatory footnotes by future scholars, but in their topical contribution to a changing sense of history and taste. The years 1948-56 are, in the Biennale's history, different from the years since. The earlier time was hectic and heroic; the profile of the twentieth century, as it still stands, was in formation. The extent to which the Venice shows were improvised can be seen by comparison with the publications of the Museum of Modern Art, New York, such as those on Italian art in 1949 and on German in 1957. The publications are useful references, the range of loans to the Museum is very wide, and the judgment of key works is more reliable than at the Biennale. These differences are normal between a unified museum organization and the multi-cell structure of the Biennale and do not abolish the significance of art history at Venice after the war.

The awkwardness of the organizational problem can be seen by the dilation of theme in the 1954 Biennale. The Secretary General requested participating countries to adhere to the central theme of Surrealism or at least to a subplot of fantastic art. The Biennale itself put on shows of Arp (fig. 87), Ernst, and Miró; Germany included Klee in its choice, England exhibited Francis Bacon, the Belgian pavilion surveyed fantastic Flanders from Bosch to Magritte—and the French pavilion showed Courbet. If there is one artist basic to any definition of *realism* it must be Courbet. One of the most-discussed works in the exhibition was Renato Guttuso's *Roman Boogie-Woogie,* a caricature-realist attack on the influence of American culture

137
THE
AVANT-GARDE
IN
A
GOLDFISH
BOWL
1948-68

(and apparently on Dutch abstract art). The subject is teen-agers jitterbugging in front of a blown-up detail of a Mondrian painting. In a situation involving diverse people in numerous countries with divergent notions of cooperation, and the sudden flips of public interest, such things will happen.

There was, of course, an abundance of new art being shown at Venice, and some of it was by the masters of modern art themselves. During the 1939-45 war, communications between the artists of different nations were totally suspended, and there was delay before international contacts were resumed, or rather took a new form, after the war. As a result, the new work of senior modern painters exercised a great fascination at the time; artists who had become legendary in reputation now revealed the work that had piled up in occupied Europe. In celebration of this renewal of contact, at Venice the major prize for paint-ing went to Braque in 1948 (fig. 82), Matisse in 1950 (fig. 83), Raoul Dufy in 1952 (fig. 84), Max Ernst in 1954 (fig. 86), and Jacques Villon in 1956 (fig. 88). The average age at which these artists received their prizes is seventy-three. Thus the juries were conferring honor on all those artists who had been ignored at Venice before. It should be remembered that it was the *new* work of these artists that was largely shown, so that the prize-giving should not be regarded solely as a retrospective gesture. It was one form of belief in the continuity of past and present, of the good fortune of the post-war art world to be in the presence of still-productive greatness. Modern art became increasingly the product of giants instead of eccen-trics, heroes instead of victims. The reappearance of the great names linked modern art and cultural prestige in a way that had not occurred before.

Less-known artists exhibited along with the acknowledged great. In 1948 in the French pavilion Braque had for company Maurice Estève, Leon Gischia, Alfred Manessier, and Edouard Pignon. They were part of a generation of synthesizing artists who wanted to combine Cubism and Matisse, nature references and formal pattern. Their effort to reconcile these diverse pos-sibilities was paralleled by the Italian *Fronte Nuovo dell'Arte,* also shown in 1948. It included Giuseppe Santomaso and Emilio Vedova, among others. That same year, in the Danish pavilion, there was a group of artists who also crossed the stylistic boundaries of earlier mordern art (Eiler Bille, Egill Jacobsen, Richard Mortensen, Carl-Henning Pedersen). Whereas the French and Italian painters made decorative signs that were *half*-cubist, *half*-coloristic, the Danish contribution (unnoticed at the time) was very different. Theirs was basically an expressionist art which used the rest of modern art as a source of forms. It appropriated elements of other styles, but did not engage in the balancing projects of the synthesists. This group, in the following year, became part of the *Cobra* movement, a North European parallel to the expressionist and surrealist fusions of American art of the 40's.

The American pavilion was as fragmented in 1948 as before the war, despite a request from Palluchini to participating countries to concentrate on a few artists at a time rather than to try and cover the field. Gorky (a work of 1938), Rothko (a watercolor), Mark Tobey (*Broadway*), Darrell Austin, and Raphael Soyer were among the crowd shown. However, there was a way to see American art in Europe in 1948: Peggy Guggenheim, who left New York and returned to Europe as soon as possible after the war, had settled in Venice, and her collection was housed as part of the Biennale in the Pavilion of Decorative Arts. The important representation was of Pollock, and included pre-drip paintings such as *Two, Moon Woman, Circumcision,* and *Eyes in the Heat.* This group was seen in Venice, as Peggy Guggenheim has recorded, by "a young Scottish painter who works like Pollock—it is funny to be influenced by Pollock instead of by Picasso—that just shows how time is marching on." [5] The artist was Alan Davie, hiking through Europe, the first of a series of encounters British artists were to have with American art.

That the post-war discovery of modern art as art history was a dominant theme at Venice is confirmed by other prizes of the period. Henry Moore won a sculpture prize in 1948, by which time he was already an official figure in British art, the equiva-

139

THE
AVANT-GARDE
IN
A
GOLDFISH
BOWL
1948-68

lent of the moderate modernism of Marino Marini (fig. 85) and Giacomo Manzù, also prize winners. Prizes went in 1950 to Zadkine and Carrà, in 1952 to Calder and Nolde, and in 1954 to Arp and Miró (the prize list also contains less eminent names, usually Italian). To achieve such coverage in the ten years after the end of World War II is clear evidence of the existence of a new, solid, cosmopolitan art world. Attendance at the first of the new Biennales, spurred by the easing of travel restrictions, and by a sense of occasion at the famous institution's renewal, was 216,471. Since then attendance has been between 150,000 and 183,000.

After the war there was a great shortage of information about what artists were doing. Art magazines, and their writers, were unequipped to deal with the problem, and exhibitions were not yet the rapid and frequent medium of transmission that they have become. The art world of Europe in the late 40's and early 50's must be pictured as full of artists out of touch with one another, conscious of waiting to see Pollock or Giacometti or Dubuffet for the first time. Not only new artists, but celebrated ones, from Arp to Vantongerloo, were unknown or little known in the original. This situation did not exist in the United States, where war had not closed the museums and condemned the galleries to show endlessly the artists of the country. (On the contrary, many European artists took refuge in the United States.) Thus the Biennale, as it showed the heroes and movements of modern art, contributed to a necessary raising of the level of information about art.

While art historical acts of conscience were being made, the organizers in Venice and the national Commissioners were turning increasingly to current art. There are important artists who have eluded, and continue to dodge, the Venice Biennale and such affairs, but they are very few. The American pavilion, after its miserable history, showed in 1950 three drip paintings by Pollock, four black-and-white paintings by de Kooning, and five Gorkys. The fact that they went unnoticed counts for less than the fact that Pollock's and de Kooning's works, then only a year or two old, were shown promptly. (The star of the pavilion, by the way, was John Marin with fifty-five works.) In 1952 the British pavilion presented a group of new sculptors, with critical and commercial success; four years and two Biennales later, one of them, Lynn Chadwick (fig. 89), won the principal sculpture prize. By 1956 the shift of emphasis is appreciable: art history is taken more for granted and the stress is on new art.

An immense number of Italian artists, with an average representation of three works, have been shown in the Central Pavilion since the war. Artists like Birolli, Corpora, Dova, Fabbri, Minguzzi, Morlotti, Scialoja, all present in 1950, are characteristic. These are not, candidly, the names of men who (writing twenty years later) can be seen to have contributed to Italian or international art. Afro, Renato Guttuso, and Emilio Vedova were also shown in 1950, and though these artists in different ways seem victims of an historical situation, they at least have clear identities as artists. Italy was in a comparatively privileged relation to the art of the times, but, in retrospect, its post-war art is unimpressive. Imagine, therefore, what the 1952 exhibition of Egypt (not yet the United Arab Republic), with over fifty artists, was like. A part of the problem is that modern art in the years 1947-54 was in a state of transition. The twentieth-century art that the Biennale was properly documenting as history was, in fact, the past. Younger artists using modern styles divided into those who tried to continue, in synthetic form, aspects of the School of Paris, and those discontented artists who rejected this route. The emergent style had, or was acquiring, names like Abstract Expressionism and "Action Painting" in the United States, or *Tachisme, l'Art informel,* and, revealingly, *l'Art autré* in Europe. Even if the change of attitude that produced the new art was hard to define, the conviction that it was something else, that it was "other," was strong. The only Italian consistently shown at Venice who worked in this direction was Lucio Fontana; he had numerous followers but none of them related cogently to his art.

Most of the new art of the Biennale came out of the conservative esthetics of the period. Earlier it was argued that the

141

THE
AVANT-GARDE
IN
A
GOLDFISH
BOWL
1948-68

late Salon artists have their place in a general theory of modern art. It is a requirement of this position that artists be compared only in a relevant context. It is possible to compare bath scenes by Gérôme and Lawrence Alma-Tadema, for instance, and find reasons for preferring Gérôme. In the same way, on the basis of comparing objects sufficiently alike, the luxuriant grids and floral analogies of conservative abstract art (say, Manessier) can be compared with the "Action-Tachiste" complex. Certainly both styles are highly painterly, but the conservative moderns lack sophistication (in their relation to the rest of art) and vigor (in the structure of their own paintings). Provided that comparisons pertain to relatable works of art they are helpful in evaluation, but comparing Gérôme and Pollock, say, is pointless.

As the Biennale became a significant factor in the spreading of knowledge and shaping of taste, national identity gained in importance in the Giardini. Each pavilion continues to be nationally administered, of course, and the competitive element of earlier years has come into the open. It was in this third phase of the Biennale that the pavilions began to be supplied with their own catalogues. Now, in addition to the compressed and comprehensive catalogue *sold* by the Agency, there are, for early visitors, illustrated—and sometimes handsome—national catalogues which are free. Here the themes of tourism and prestige are compounded: these are not only the Biennale's chief values to the city of Venice, they are also the inducement to the participating countries, who pay all their own expenses. Costs vary with the labor situation in each country and with its distance from Venice, but a minimum budget for the American pavilion in the early 60's would be $30,000. Investments of this order can be justified in terms of national reputation. The Spanish and British pavilions, for example, successfully reached a big audience in ways that earned national credit as well as benefiting the artists who moved at a new speed into the international scene. There are critics with moral objections to such exposure, but why is it better for artists to work obscurely, and hence in ignorance of one another, than for them to work in the knowledge of everybody else's activity?

The definition of the recent past and the present requires a sense of timing as well as an eye. Consider post-war sculpture styles, which crystallized in a 1952 group show in the British pavilion. By the end of that decade, the qualities implicit or stated earlier, texture and anthropomorphism, were internationally abundant. The 1960 Biennale displayed work in that style in the American, Austrian, Brazilian, British, Swiss, Yugoslavian, and Central pavilions. There were monsters, personages, patinated Silly Symphony hybrids, and giant jewelry everywhere.[6] This was the year in which the Austrian sculptor Rudolf Hoflehner charmed the collectors, with the Yugoslav Dzamonja a close second. Hoflehner's split human image was as shallow and decorative as Lynn Chadwick's kite-like figures, and Dzamonja made ornaments with creepy larval references. Seeing it all together made it possible to decide that here was a period style that had lost the crispness of its origins (for example, Theodore Roszak's work in the 40's) and the freshness of its appearance in the early 50's. Its decadence was not accelerated or brought about by big exhibitions, obviously; what the Biennale did was reveal, by giving the chance for comparative judgment, the state of the style. The exposure was not, of course, planned, but an accidental revelation arising from the separate national Commissioners' plans. Obviously Commissioners are torn between reliability and novelty, proven performance and impact, in their choice of artists, and 1960 provides a clear case of their staying too long with a momentary style.

A success story of the Biennale (and of São Paulo and Pittsburgh) is that of Spanish art. It started in 1952 when Antonio Tàpies was one of thirty artists shown. Other painters who were adopted by dealers and collectors from later Biennales are Rafael Canogar, Modest Cuixart, Luis Feito, Manuel Millares, Antonio Saura, and J. J. Tharrats. The Spanish, owing to the purposeful monotony of their artists, have revealed exceptional skill in projecting a unified national image. In 1950, before the appearance of notable individuals, the pavilion was devoted to a group show of "Black and White Paintings." The artists

143

THE
AVANT-GARDE
IN
A
GOLDFISH
BOWL
1948-68

who showed subsequently stayed pretty much within these
limits. Their dark and textured works shared an image of romantic Spain as parched, dark, and tragic. One of the objections
of critics hostile to big shows has been that they encourage an
internationalism which ruthlessly flattens precious local qualities
in art. This argument is used in good faith by organicist critics
and expediently by writers merely opposed to whatever the
dominant current style might be. However, Spanish unanimity
of color and image seems less the result of national character
appearing spontaneously than of the deliberate cultivation of
a concept of Spain to service a style of painting. It is re-nationalization more than nationalism; affective national cues, such as
late Goya and the uncultivated landscape, the Spanish Civil War
and the bullfight, are used by artists already in possession of an
international style.

"What I learned in Paris is *leaving me*," Van Gogh wrote in
1888. "I am returning to the ideas I had in the country before
I knew the impressionists." [7] Emile Bernard commented that
Van Gogh was "re-becoming Dutch," but, of course, he had
been changed by his Paris period. It is in this sense that I speak
of re-nationalization in modern art. The shared formal characteristics of the post-war Spanish painters are pretty brittle as
evidence of roots and national temperament. It was, however,
a most serviceable fusion of individual handling (personal art)
with agreed-on emblems for "Spain" (public art). Perhaps the
separation of international and national qualities in recent art
is an archaic system of classification. With the increase of both
knowledge of art and of self-knowledge among artists, much
of what is decisive in art cannot be analyzed nationally. Even
artists who stress local properties (as have Danish artists also)
are re-nationalizing as an act of choice and not acting merely
as the Motherland's unconscious agent. For instance, Tàpies,
the sole substantial Spanish painter in my opinion, was influenced by Jean Dubuffet and Fontana when he began to thicken
his paint and cut into it. These French and Italian connections
are as much a part of his art as the Spanish atmosphere that has
been attached to it. This is a situation that is beyond a simple

polarity of native virtue and alien tradition, sincerity with roots versus *déraciné* fashion.

1958 was the year in which there was an appreciable shift away from art that was in suspense between historically-defined style and emergent possibility. Fontana (fig. 39) showed a group of large, dark paintings perforated by rows and scatters of small holes. (These were his last paintings with multiple openings; in reaction against his success at the Biennale he began the large slashes in completely monochrome canvases.) Elsewhere in the Central Pavilion a retrospective exhibition of Wols provided the first chance for many interested people to see a sizable sample of paintings and drawings by this pioneer of the *Informel*. Mark Rothko (end paper) was one of four artists in the American pavilion. This was the first Biennale I saw, and I can remember the effect of Fontana, Wols, and Rothko combined. This is not a grouping one would make now, but at the time all that was clear was that these artists were different from what had gone before and hence part of the *Informel*-Abstract Expressionist-*l'Art autré* cluster.

When Fautrier slapped Franz Kline or Kline socked Fautrier in 1960, a new theme had appeared at the Biennale: the relation of American and European art. The problem would have come up earlier if the American pavilion had been handled more strongly by its Commissioners, because the art certainly existed in New York. As it was, a European desire to concentrate on its own art remained more or less undisturbed. Earlier American shows never hit on the right artist in sufficient quantity at the right time; it amounted almost to a kind of accidental collaboration with the European desire to ignore American art. In addition, the American artists lacked dealers working on their behalf to create a climate of anticipation. Although Fautrier was the one felled in the encounter with Kline, it was Fautrier who won the main prize for painting (fig. 92). He had had a chain of exhibitions around Europe for years prior to the show, ample advertising in the magazines as the summer approached, and he had a literature that included texts by André Malraux and Francis Ponge. Nobody had seen Kline's

145

THE
AVANT-GARDE
IN
A
GOLDFISH
BOWL
1948-68

work before and there was nothing to read about him. (Significantly, the Sidney Janis gallery, which represented Kline and most of the Abstract Expressionists at this time, did not start putting out illustrated catalogues regularly until 1960.) If we regard the Biennale as part of a loop of information, we can ascribe some of its influence to confirmation elsewhere on the loop. However, when the loop is incomplete the jury in Venice is short of information too. Philip Guston and Hans Hofmann were in the Biennale that year with Kline, but neither of them had the visibility and status of Fautrier at that moment.[8]

In the summer of 1962 the Galleria d'Arte Moderna in Venice exhibited works by the prize winners of the post-war Biennales, a reminder of that museum's close relation. In 1897 Alberto Giovanelli offered works he had purchased at the Biennale to the City and exerted polite pressure on the Syndic. He argued that Venice was well-endowed with museums of the past, but lacked a gallery for modern art. He was right, and though the gallery was founded, Venice still needs a modern art museum. A Venetian bank, the hotels, the Chamber of Commerce, individual citizens, and King Vittorio Emanuele III supported Giovanelli's project. The museum opened in 1902 at the Palazzo Pesaro, where it still languishes. Directed at first by the Secretary General of the Biennale, it was given its first full-time director in 1907, Nino Barbantini. Years later he reappears on the Commission of the Biennale after World War II. In the decades between he had successfully resisted what he termed in his book "the Labyrinth" of modern art. As late as 1950 there was a Favretto exhibition in the Biennale, and inevitably, the text was Barbantini's. The optimism with which the gallery was started is not justified by the meagre resources and bleak display of the Ca' Pesaro today. It is curious, considering the amount of new art that arrives in Venice every two years, that no way has been found to retain adequate examples in the city.

In the first eleven Biennales an average of fifteen countries participated (the actual range was from twelve to nineteen).

For the next twelve Biennales the average was down to thirteen (out of a range of ten to twenty-three). Finally, in the ten Biennales from 1948 to 1966 an average of thirty countries have exhibited (out of a range of fifteen to thirty-seven). These figures reveal clearly the Fascist withdrawal and then the new scale of post-war internationalism. The presence of more countries has not, on the whole, revealed new artists or new traditions. Nonetheless, Argentina and Japan are both producing original work (neither Folk Art nor Oriental in type) and there is no reason to suppose that more will not come from the Biennale's newcomers. As things stand at present, however, the game is still between the same countries as before. In the 1962 Biennale Giacometti and Manessier received the main prizes and visitors could see Louis Moillet (the Swiss artist who went to Tunisia with Klee), Riopelle (representing Canada where he was born, not France where he lives), Gorky (an Armenian emigrant to the United States), and Hundertwasser for Austria. Hundertwasser is a case of re-nationalization inasmuch as Klimt and Schiele references recur persistently in his art. The accumulation of such national crossovers is like a preliminary global culture; every country does not contribute to it as a producer, but it is available generally in terms of consumption. An international style is not necessarily the product of every country, but one that is accessible to the understanding of any country.

It is noticeable that much of the art shown at Venice in the early 60's was established to the point of over-familiarity. Too much was an evocation or an extension of the styles of the immediate post-war period. Even Giacometti (fig. 93), seen apart from the French existentialist criticism originated for him by Sartre, did not induce that old feeling, though, of course, the prize was richly deserved. The improvement in the level of knowledge of current art to which the Biennale itself has contributed so much has caught up with it. Obviously the Biennale could not afford to be identified with one generation, however good some of its members might be. 1964 was the year in which the emphasis of the Biennale shifted to include a substantial number of artists working in post-*Informel* or post-

147

THE
AVANT-GARDE
IN
A
GOLDFISH
BOWL
1948-68

Abstract Expressionist styles. The prestige of abstract art, once so hard to establish, now prompted resistance to a new form of figurative art. A return to the figure had been expected for years after the war, especially in Italy, by communists and by critics who were experts in the Human Condition and the difficulty of being a man. This mesh of political and/or existentialist ideas, however, never extended very far beyond Guttuso. Instead, abstract painting, often in lush painterly form, was abundant and cheap in Italy. The Pop Artists, however, rejected the fiction of a national facture (Mediterranean sensuality revealed in messy color) and all tended, in one way or another, to a diagrammatic crispness. In the Central Pavilion were Lucio del Pezzo's three-dimensional illusionist still lifes, Tano Festa's copies of Michelangelo's Adam and hand of God from the Sistine Ceiling spaced out over slightly parted panels, Franco Angeli's anti-American symbols, Antonio Recalcati's paintings, which look as if James Rosenquist were illustrating Graham Greene's London. In short, Italian Pop Art was out in the open. Mimmo Rotella's *décollage,* mostly large torn posters, was shown; the European parallel and rival to Pop Art, New Realism, was thus also present. Gruppo N and Gruppo T, collaboratives of artists who wanted to efface individual authorship, also exhibited small walk-in environments defined by light control and moving parts. These installations were tucked away on the Canal di Sant'Elena side of the Pavilion, which is not a prime location, but it is their presence that counts.

The first phase of the Biennale increased the exposure of new works, a tendency that had been continuous, though not rapid, since the eighteenth century. Between the wars the tendency was diverted, as many of the conspicuous artists at Venice were working in forms of public art, pre-set iconography, and competitions. In the third phase of the Biennale there has been a return to the original premise of the organizers, namely, the prompt exhibition of private art, of work done without prior commission and without limits set externally. As the art historical shows shaded off and newly-done work dominated the pavilions, the artist and his audience moved closer. The patterns of alienation and distance, by which modern artists had defined earlier relations with the public, became inadequate models of behavior. As increasing numbers of new works are revealed and instantly discussed or purchased, the artist is separated from his work in the same way that a writer gets separated from the form of his ideas as they are circulated. This split, physical or ideological, between an artist and his art dematerializes the work for its maker even as it becomes more solid to the audience. It is an experience like this, I think, which underlies artists' suspicions of the media that love them and on which they depend.

Paintings and sculptures, unless they are collaborative or contracted to workshops for execution, are made in the studio, which is traditionally defined as somewhere between a laboratory and a forum for the artist's friends. As such it was presumed private, but this seclusion has been reduced. Photographers record the contents of studios and the development of particular works. The artist, therefore, is displayed in action, as close to the creative act as photographs of astronauts, monarchs, and suicides show them close to their acts. Apart from this documentation, for twenty years after the war, in Europe and the United States, esthetics stressed process, the act of making art. Thus the artist entered the mass media, as well as the art journals and catalogues, as a professional *at work*. It must be remembered that, operationally, modern artists are not too different from other post-Renaissance artists. The studios of Fontana and Rauschenberg, Braque and Pollock, are not very different from Velasquez's and Chardin's. They are the special zones where art objects are made, with a personally-scaled technology devoted to the artist's maximum control. The technical level of art, in terms of man and tools, has not changed much; work in the studio is still mainly empirical and art the product of trial and error. This is, naturally, a source of the sense of the solidity of his art that an artist feels. Suddenly, however, any artist may acquire a global context, without any mediating routine.

The avant-garde has become a subject of immediate interest

149

THE
AVANT-GARDE
IN
A
GOLDFISH
BOWL
1948-68

and scrutiny. A one-man exhibition in a gallery reaches comparatively few people, though it is a highly influential group. A review of the show in an art magazine reaches, at most, 15,000 people, most of whom will not see the show, but know the artist's name and work. General magazines carry images and news of the avant-garde everywhere and attendance at the Biennale is steady around 174,000. Thus the avant-garde is in a goldfish bowl, with the studio opened up and the work distributed instantly to crowds. New trends are measured as sensitively as shifts in the San Andreas Fault. The term avant-garde, so potent to intellectuals as recently as the 40's, is obsolete. The alignment of art and news services, while it does not reduce the specialized content of new work, exposes the "advanced" to a "mass" without rejection. Artists' statements, reproductions, reviews, admit anybody who is interested to new art. We can even expect to have information, which would once have remained private, about national Commissioners during the jury's decision-making at Venice. "Alan Solomon pulled me aside and said in a tight voice: 'The judges [*sic*] have just voted four to three for Rauschenberg on the basis of one painting at the Biennale grounds. But the president of the jury has threatened to resign in protest, and they're going to try to work out something tomorrow.' " [9]

The award of the prize to Robert Rauschenberg in 1964 confirmed the shift away from post-war abstract art. Inevitably it was also treated as a combat of American art against European, as well as a political drama. The Museum of Modern Art had administered the pavilion from 1948 to 1962 but relinquished it owing to funding problems. The United States Information Agency took it over and appointed Alan Solomon, then Director of the Jewish Museum, as Commissioner. He decided on a partial survey of the period 1955-60, concentrating on Rauschenberg and Jasper Johns, on the one hand, and Morris Louis and Kenneth Noland, on the other. That is to say, either artists with the Leo Castelli Gallery or artists sponsored by Clement Greenberg. (There were additional artists but they were perfunctorily shown.) The scale of the projected show exceeded the capacity of the American pavilion. The Biennale authorities refused Solomon's request for extra space in the Central Pavilion, but were understood to have agreed to a spill-over section off the grounds. The big paintings of Louis and Noland occupied the pavilion and the other artists were housed in the former U.S. Consulate. Then, while the jury was considering the awards, Solomon learned that the Biennale would not accept the works in the Consulate building as eligible. Noland refused to give up any of his half of the pavilion, and Louis, as a recently deceased painter constantly linked with the younger Noland, could hardly be cut back, even if the widow and her adviser (Greenberg) were to agree.

Solomon's solution was to improvise a temporary exhibition structure in the court of the pavilion for a token work by each artist. The erection of this Pop Art patio was urgent, because Rauschenberg was emerging as a likely winner. Finally, to satisfy the president of the jury, three additional Rauschenberg paintings were added. The prize was decided before the extra pictures were brought to the pavilion, but it was clearly necessary to rationalize the situation; otherwise the top prize would have gone to an artist virtually missing from the Giardini. The arrangement looked like the expedient it was, with the prize winner squeezed outside by the vast, overlooked paintings within. There were the usual vague allegations of jury tampering, but these ignore the fact that a favorable predisposition towards Rauschenberg's art already existed in Europe, as well as an indigenous European Pop movement. The fact that an American won the prize was a shock to some art establishments, but it was well received by many artists and writers. Rauschenberg was thirty-nine when he got the prize (just under the symbolic line of forty) and it was taken as recognition by the Biennale of a younger generation and newer syles. Pierre Restany, for example, regarded Rauschenberg's prize as sign of a turn to "a closer and more accurate survey of the young generation and experimental research work." [10]

It is a habit of the avant-garde to describe art as "experimental research work," but there are difficulties, because *research*

151

THE
AVANT-GARDE
IN
A
GOLDFISH
BOWL
1948-68

has a prior target or direction and results can be verified by other researchers, which is not so in art. There is a difference between cumulative knowledge, which is like a snowball that gets bigger, and, as it were, more right, the longer it rolls, and noncumulative knowledge,[11] which is neither progressive nor checkable. Indeed, it is a confusion between these two types of knowledge that may underlie the rigidity of writers who hanker for scientific criticism. However, there is no doubt that Restany was correct in seeing, and welcoming, a new emphasis. He listed for praise Oyvind Fahlström, Martial Raysse, Roy Lichtenstein, Julio Le Parc, Ay-O, Fontana, del Pezzo, and Pistoletto. Ay-O's *Tactile Room* (fig. 41) is one of the first multi-sense art works to be seen in the Biennale (rainbow color and invitation to touch) and certainly a sign of many environmental displays to come. The shift was caused partly by the weakness of gestural and sensual abstract art itself, which had not been strongly sustained by many artists. Partly it was caused by the mounting interest in alternative ways of working; this was revealed in 1963 when the 4th International Biennale of San Marino took as its theme "Beyond the *Informel*." Restany was on the committee and so was Umbro Apollonio of the Venice Biennale. Gruppo N and Gruppo T were invited to San Marino and so, among others, were Raysse, Rauschenberg, Johns, Lichtenstein (to list only artists seen at the next two Venice Biennales).

There must have been, also, an increasing obligation among the Biennale's organizers toward a new generation of artists. There have always been prodigies, but never before has it been normal for art to be a successful product of the young. As a result there is no set age now at which an artist is said to be "ready in terms of his development" to show. The moment varies, and timing is as much social as it is esthetic. Rauschenberg seemed like a young prize winner, the way John F. Kennedy seemed like a young President (though Pitt was Prime Minister of England in his early twenties). One might say that Rauschenberg did not get a prize at Venice *until* he was thirty-nine and that he should have had such honors sooner. In fact, a decade earlier, when he was making combines like *Charlene, Bed,* and *Satellite,* a prize would have been marvelously timed, inasmuch as this work is stronger and more complex than the silk-screen paintings he was doing at the time of the Venice show. On the other hand, when the prize is given later rather than earlier, it is more obviously *earned,* which is one of the social expectations that has to be satisfied.

It should not be thought that the Biennale of Venice has turned into a Paris Biennale, which has an upper age limit of thirty-five. What has happened is that the Biennale has been adaptive and has accommodated post-*Informel* art, the way it earlier absorbed (after initial delay) the *Informel.* Various generations and styles are present as before, as a check of the other prize winners of 1964 shows. Kemeny, a heavy decorative sculptor (Swiss), balanced the painting prize. Andrea Cascella and Arnaldo Pomodoro both received sculpture prizes, presumably as the older and younger ends of the middle generation; the German Joseph Fassbender and Angelo Savelli, a sophisticated engraver, also won prizes. These prizes, however, were not the subject of dissent, only the one awarded Rauschenberg, who is, incidentally, the only artist in the list in whom I place confidence.

It is the status or fate of the avant-garde to work in a goldfish bowl, a situation that is not likely to be reversed or reduced. This could only happen if there were a withdrawal of public interest, and that seems out of the question. The audience for direct contact with art, in museums at home, in extravaganzas like the Biennale, will not be lost, because the education and society that developed the audience's taste is unlikely to change. The only change to expect, in fact, must be a bigger audience. Museum personnel do not seem to be departing from the view of history on which the involvement of museums with current art rests. If the discontent with galleries that artists express leads to anything, it is more likely to add another channel of distribution to those already existing than to destroy the "gallery system." Artists as personalities or artists in newsworthy situations are themes renewable in the mass media with each

153

THE
AVANT-GARDE
IN
A
GOLDFISH
BOWL
1948-68

generation of artists, and with each generation of readers and viewers.

The problem facing the Biennale, and other giant shows, is to preserve its function against other channels of communication. Such exhibitions are most effective where there is a gap in the public knowledge of art. In Argentina, for example, there is an audience big enough and uninformed enough to benefit strongly from such shows. The Instituto Torcuato Di Tella in Buenos Aires has held international and national prize shows annually since 1960, with an appreciable influence on art and taste in the country. Such exhibitions benefit the artists as well. In Cordoba, since 1962, the Bienal Americana de Arte (subsidized by Industrias Kaiser Argentina) has shown South American artists to each other. As there is little cross-communication of ideas between Latin American countries, this function is timely.

The Venice Biennale and other media have reduced our ignorance about twentieth-century art. Thus, in future, anthologies or compilations on the past model will not be sufficient to hold either specialists or the wider public. Greater control of exhibitions, so that relevant themes can be cogently displayed, may be necessary, though obviously this will present difficulties, given the Biennale's cellular structure. (Courbet's appearance in the Surrealist-oriented Biennale of 1954 indicates the obstacle the structure presents.) The problem for the Biennale now is to work out a control system to replace *laissez-faire,* without losing cooperation of the thirty-seven nations that participated in 1966.

1. The "Commissione per l'arte figurativa" consisted of: Giovanni Ponti, Rodolfo Palluchini, Nino Barbantini, Carlo Carrà, Felice Casorati, Roberto Longhi, Marino Marini, Giorgio Morandi, Carlo Ludovico Ragghianti, Pio Semeghini, Lionello Venturi. In 1950 they were joined by Giuseppe Fiocco, Leoncillo Leonardi, Giacomo Manzù. The committee is drawn from art historians and established modern artists, to confer stability on the new phase. Romolo Bazzoni continues as consultant.

2. Catalogue, XXIV Biennale, 1958.

3. Once the idea of a neutral zone between past and present, to hold the past at a fixed distance, is abandoned, consider what is entailed. It follows (1) that the uncertainties of the present can corrode the meaning of past events, and (2) that the present can be the subject of the same scrupulous and searching techniques that historians bring to the past. Thus, the amount of work and the uncertainty of the result both increase. It is history without a cut-off point.

4. This tendency is not restricted to temporary exhibitions: it can be seen in museums and books. The Museum of Modern Art's catalogues by Alfred H. Barr are organized on the basis of data-collection, and Christian Zervos' *catalogue raisonné* of Picasso was started in the 1920's. In both cases the techniques of art history are being applied to living artists. Objectivity becomes an expression of faith in the value of knowledge about art and in the living artist. Much of the criticism of modern exhibitions and catalogues, incidentally, seems to derive less from a dislike of modern *styles* than from resistance to the application of objective criteria to the complex present.

5. Peggy Guggenheim, letter to Betty Parsons.

6. Lawrence Alloway, "Notes on Sculpture, Venice Biennale, 1960," *Architectural Design* (London), XXX, No. 11 (1960).

7. Vincent Van Gogh, *The Letters of Van Gogh,* Mark Roskill, ed. (New York, 1963).

155
THE
AVANT-GARDE
IN
A
GOLDFISH
BOWL
1948-68

8. For the record, Fautrier's reputation waned rapidly; this is interesting, for it suggests that the prize, though confirmatory of a high level of interest, as a rule cannot save declining artists or divert changing tastes.

9. Calvin Tomkins, "The Big Show in Venice," *Harper's Magazine,* CCXXX, No. 1379 (1965). Most of the subsequent account of Rauschenberg at the Biennale is from this source.

10. Pierre Restany, "L'Uomo Luedens contre l'Homme Faber," *Domus,* August, 1966.

11. Crane Brinton, *Ideas and Man* (New York, 1950). Quoted by William S. Beck in *Modern Science and the Nature of Life* (New York, 1957).

PRIZE WINNERS

42. Francesco Paolo Michetti. *The Daughter of Jorio.*
1895, Premio della Città di Venezia.

Note: The date of execution is given only if it is significantly
earlier than the Biennale in which the work was exhibited. Medium
is oil, tempera, or plastic paint on canvas unless otherwise indicated.

43. Alessandro Milesi. *Marriage.*
1897, Premio del Municipio di Venezia.
44. Emilio Marsili. *The Happy Age* (bronze).
1897, Premio del Governo (divided with Anders Zorn).

5. Anders Zorn. *In a Beerhouse*. 1897, Premio del
Governo (divided with Emi-
lo Marsili).
6. Giulio Aristide Sartorio.
*The Gorgon and her He-
roes*. 1897, Acquisition prize.
7. Luigi Selvatico. *Early
Morning Departure*. 1897,
Acquisition prize.
8. Domencio Trentacoste.
Daughter of Niobe. 1897,
Acquisition prize.
9. Telemaco Signorini. *Lunatic Asylum for Women*.
1901, Acquisition prize.

50. Luigi Nono. *First Steps* (1876). 1901, Acquisition prize.
51. Emile Claus. *A Flemish Kitchen Garden*. 1903, Acquisition prize.
52. Gaston La Touche. *Death of the Faun*. 1903, Acquisition prize.
53. Franz von Lenbach. *Regent of Bavaria*. 1903, Acquisition prize.
54. Herman Anglada-Camarasa. *The Elysian Fields*. 1905, one of ten Gold Medals.

55. Károly Ferenczy. *Self-Portrait.*
1905, one of ten Gold Medals.
56. Philip Laszlo. *Portrait of My Wife.*
1907, one of thirteen Gold Medals.
57. Jozef Israels. *High Tide.*
1907, one of thirteen Gold Medals.

58. John Singer Sargent. *The Acheson Sisters.*
1907, one of thirteen Gold Medals.
59. Hans von Bartels. *Dutch Milkmaid.*
1912, Premio Dreber.
60. Adolfo de Karolis. *Women on the Shore.*
1914, Premio della Città di Chioggia.

61. Giuseppe Biase. *Girls of Osile*.
1920, Premio Opera Nazionale Combattenti (divided with
Giuseppe Zanetti).
62. Giuseppe Zanetti. *Maternity* (marble).
1920, Premio Opera Nazionale Combattenti (divided with
Giuseppe Biase).
63. Albin Egger-Lienz. *The Meal*.
1922, Premio del Comune di Venezia.
64. Max Liebermann. *Cabbage Fields*.
1922, Premio Dreber.
65. Primo Conti. *Christ among the Doctors*.
1924, Premio della *Gazzetta di Venezia*.
66. Armando Spadini. *Husband and Wife*.
1924, Premio Fondazione Reverdin.

67. Fioravente Seibezzi. *Burano*.
1926, Premio Marini-Missani
(divided with Michele Guerrisi).
68. Michele Guerrisi. *Nude* (plaster).
1926, Premio Marini-Missani
(divided with Fioravente Seibezzi).
69. Arnaldo Carpanetti. *Incipit Novus Ordo*.
1930, Premio del Partito Nazionale Fascista.
70. Amerigo Canegrati. *Mother*.
1930, Premio della Città di Venezia
(for maternity subjects).
71. Gherardo Dottori. *Anno X*.
1932, Premio del Ministero Corporazioni
(divided with Alfio Paolo Graziani and
Tommaso Cascella).

72. Alfio Paolo Graziani. *Anno X.* 1932, Premio del Ministero Corporazioni (divided with Gherardo Dottori and Tommaso Cascella).

73. Tommaso Cascella. *Anno X.* 1932, Premio del Ministerio Corporazioni (divided with Gherardo Dottori and Alfio Paolo Graziani).

74. Contardo Barbieri. *Giorni di Adunata* (detail). 1934, Premio del Partito Nazionale Fascista (divided with Manlio Giarrizzo).

75. Manlio Giarrizzo. *Il Duce at Littoria*. 1934, Premio del Partito Nazionale Fascista (divided with Contardo Barbieri).

76. Giovanni Barbisan. *Our Best Friends are the Peasants*. 1936, one of eight winners of a Fresco Competition.

77. Ezio Buscio. *Giovanni Berta.* 1936, one of eight winners of a Fresco Competition.
78. Ignazio Zuloaga. *Belmonte.* 1938, Premio di Duce.
79. Felice Casorati. *Nude in an Armchair.* 1938, Premio del Comune di Venezia.
80. Guglielmo Aba-Novák. *Yoked Bulls.* 1940, Premio del Capo del Governo.
81. Artur Kampf. *The People's Offering.* 1942, Premio del Capo del Governo.

82. Georges Braque. *The Chair.*
1948, Premio Presidenza del Consiglio dei Ministri.
83. Henri Matisse. *Still Life with Magnolias.*
1950, Premio Presidenza Consiglio dei Ministri.
84. Raoul Dufy. *Studio.*
1952, Premio Presidenza Consiglio dei Ministri.

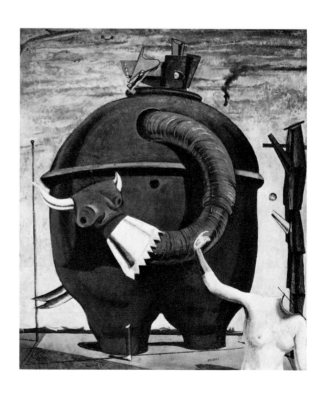

85. Marino Marini. *Grande Cavallo*. 1954, Premio del Comune di Venezia.

86. Max Ernst. *Celebes* (1921). 1954, Premio Presidenza Consiglio dei Ministri.

87. Jean Arp. *L'Orologio* (painted wood, 1924). 1954, Premio Presidenza Consiglio dei Ministri.

88. Jacques Villon. *Bridge at Beaugincy* (1944). 1956, Premio Presidenza Consiglio dei Ministri.

89. Lynn Chadwick. *The Inner Eye* (metal and glass). 1956, Premio Presidenza Consiglio dei Ministri.
90. Osvaldo Licini. *Amalasunta*. 1958, Premio Presidenza Consiglio dei Ministri.
91. Mark Tobey. *Capricorn*. 1958, Premio del Comune di Venezia.
92. Jean Fautrier. *Wa Da Da*. 1960, Premio Presidenza Consiglio dei Ministri.
93. Alberto Giacometti. *Seated Woman* (bronze). 1962, Premio Presidenza Consiglio dei Ministri.

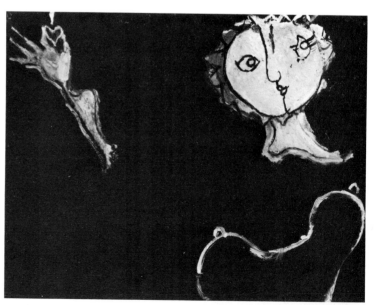

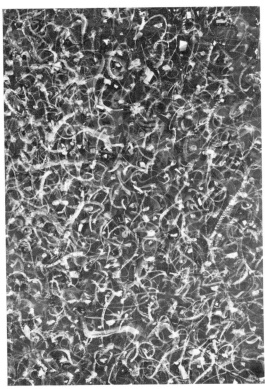

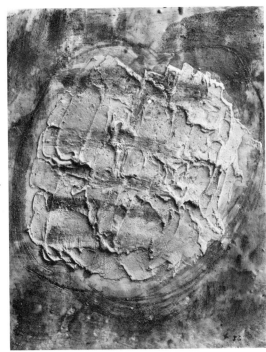

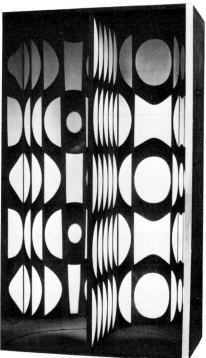

94. Robert Rauschenberg. *Buffalo II.*
1964, Premio Presidenza Consiglio dei Ministri.
95. Julio Le Parc. *Potential Circles.*
1966, Premio Presidenza Consiglio dei Ministri.

LIST OF ILLUSTRATIONS

Historical Photographs

1. Palazzo dell'Esposizione in 1895. Facade designed by Marius de Maria.
2. Palazzo dell'Esposizione in 1914. New facade designed by Guido Cirilli.
3. Palazzo dell'Esposizione. Facade in 1932, and as it appears at present, designed by Giulio Torres.
4. Poster of the First Biennale, 1895.
5. Their Majesties King Umberto I and Queen Margherita at the inauguration of the Biennale, 1895.
6. Il Duce at the Biennale, 1934.
7. Hitler at the Biennale, 1934, in the margins of a state visit to Mussolini.
8. His Majesty the King Emperor Vittorio Emanuele III (center), with F. T. Marinetti (right).
9. Giacomo Grosso. *The Last Meeting.* 1895.
10. James McNeill Whistler. *The Little White Girl. Symphony in White, no. 11.* Painted 1864, Biennale 1895.
11. International Gallery, D, at II Biennale, 1897. *The Flight of Charles the Bold after the Battle of Morat,* by Eugene Burnand.
12. Giacomo Favretto, one-man exhibition, Gallery B, at III Biennale, 1899.
13. Giacomo Favretto. *Walk in the Piazzetta.* 1899.
14. Jef Leempoels (Belgium). *The Enigma.* 1899.
15. Fernand Khnopff. *The Sleeping Medusa.* Painted 1886, Biennale 1954 (Belgian Pavilion).

16. Tuscan Gallery, 1901. *Beethoven,* by Lionello Balestrieri (left). Committee for the decoration: R. Mazzanti, F. Gioli, V. Giustiniani, D. Trentacoste.

17. Emilian Gallery, 1903. Decorations by A. Rubbiani, A. Sézanne, A. Tantarini, A. Casanova, G. Romagnoli.

18. Modern Portraits, Gallery P, 1903. Decorations by A. Tamburlini and R. Carbonaro.

19. International Galleries, 33-34, 1907. *Garibaldi* by Plinio Nomellini (center), *John the Baptist* by Galileo Chini (tondo), and *Prometheus Liberated* by Walter Crane (right).

20. Peter Severin Kröyer, one-man exhibition, 1909.

21. Gustav Klimt, one-man exhibition, 1910.

22. Ettore Tito. *Le Rappezzatrici.* 1903.

23. Ettore Tito. *The Pearl.* 1914.

24. Pietro Fragiacomo. *L'Ora della Polenta.* 1924.

25. Alessandro Milesi. *Antonio Fradeletto.* 1935.

26. Gallery in the Central Pavilion, 1928.

27. Arturo Tosi. *The Track.* 1932.

28. Carlo Carrà. *The Bathers.* 1930.

29. Riccardo Schrotter. *The Judgment of Paris.* 1924.

30. Adolfo Wildt. *Il Duce.* 1924.

31. Enrico Prampolini. *Mussolini: Plastic Synthesis.* 1926.

32. Postcard, 1930. The numerals XVII refer to the Biennale, and VIII to the Fascist calendar.

33. Postcard, 1940.

34. Futurist Gallery, 39, in the Central Pavilion, 1930.

35. S. G. Tato. *Mechanical Splendor* (in the "Aeropittori Futuristi" exhibition). 1934.

36. Enrico Prampolini. *Inhabitant of the Stratosphere.* 1932.

37. Giuseppe Virgili. *Roman Civilization* (bas-relief). 1938.

38. Renato Guttuso. *The Execution of Nicola Belojannis.* 1952.

39. Lucio Fontana. *Spatial Concept.* 1958.

40. Roy Lichtenstein. *Temple of Apollo.* 1966 (Collection of Mr. and Mrs. Robert A. Rowan).

41. Ay-O. *Tactile Room.* 1966.

Prize Winners

Note: The date of execution is given only if it is significantly earlier than the Biennale in which the work was exhibited. Medium is oil, tempera, or plastic paint on canvas unless otherwise indicated.

42. Francesco Paolo Michetti. *The Daughter of Jorio.*
    1895, Premio della Città di Venezia.
43. Alessandro Milesi. *Marriage.*
    1897, Premio del Municipio di Venezia.
44. Emilio Marsili. *The Happy Age* (bronze).
    1897, Premio del Governo (divided with Anders Zorn).
45. Anders Zorn. *In a Beerhouse.*
    1897, Premio del Governo (divided with Emilio Marsili).
46. Giulio Aristide Sartorio. *The Gorgon and Her Heroes.*
    1897, Acquisition prize.
47. Luigi Selvatico. *Early Morning Departure.*
    1897, Acquisition prize.
48. Domenico Trentacoste. *Daughter of Niobe.*
    1897, Acquisition prize.
49. Telemaco Signorini. *Lunatic Asylum for Women.*
    1901, Acquisition prize.
50. Luigi Nono. *First Steps* (1876).
    1901, Acquisition prize.
51. Emile Claus. *A Flemish Kitchen Garden.*
    1903, Acquisition prize.
52. Gaston La Touche. *Death of the Faun.*
    1903, Acquisition prize.
53. Franz von Lenbach. *Regent of Bavaria.*
    1903, Acquisition prize.
54. Herman Anglada-Camarasa. *The Elysian Fields.*
    1905, one of ten Gold Medals.
55. Károly Ferenczy. *Self-Portrait.*
    1905, one of ten Gold Medals.
56. Philip Laszlo. *Portrait of My Wife.*
    1907, one of thirteen Gold Medals.
57. Jozef Israels. *High Tide.*
    1907, one of thirteen Gold Medals.

58. John Singer Sargent. *The Acheson Sisters.*
    1907, one of thirteen Gold Medals.
59. Hans von Bartels. *Dutch Milkmaid.*
    1912, Premio Dreber.
60. Adolfo de Karolis. *Women on the Shore.*
    1914, Premio della Città di Chioggia.
61. Giuseppe Biase. *Girls of Osile.*
    1920, Premio Opera Nazionale Combattenti (divided with Giuseppe Zanetti).
62. Giuseppe Zanetti. *Maternity* (marble).
    1920, Premio Opera Nazionale Combattenti (divided with Giuseppe Biase).
63. Albin Egger-Lienz. *The Meal.*
    1922, Premio del Comune di Venezia.
64. Max Liebermann. *Cabbage Fields.*
    1922, Premio Dreber.
65. Primo Conti. *Christ among the Doctors.*
    1924, Premio della *Gazetta di Venezia.*
66. Armando Spadini. *Husband and Wife.*
    1924, Premio Fondazione Reverdin.
67. Fioravente Seibezzi. *Burano.*
    1926, Premio Marini-Missani (divided with Michele Guerrisi).
68. Michele Guerrisi. *Nude* (plaster).
    1926, Premio Marini-Missani (divided with Fioravente Seibezzi).
69. Arnaldo Carpanetti. *Incipit Novus Ordo.*
    1930, Premio del Partito Nazionale Fascista.
70. Amerigo Canegrati. *Mother.*
    1930, Premio della Città di Venezia (for maternity subjects).
71. Gherardo Dottori. *Anno X.*
    1932. Premio del Ministero Corporazioni (divided with Alfio Paolo Graziani and Tommaso Cascella).
72. Alfio Paolo Graziani. *Anno X.*
    1932, Premio del Ministero Corporazioni (divided with Gherardo Dottori and Tommaso Cascella).

73. Tommaso Cascella. *Anno X.*
   1932, Premio del Ministero Corporazioni (divided with
   Gherardo Dottori and Alfio Paolo Graziani).

74. Contardo Barbieri. *Giorni di Adunata* (detail).
   1934, Premio del Partito Nazionale Fascista (divided with
   Manlio Giarrizzo).

75. Manlio Giarrizzo. *Il Duce at Littoria.*
   1934, Premio del Partito Nazionale Fascista (divided with
   Contardo Barbieri).

76. Giovanni Barbisan. *Our Best Friends are the Peasants.*
   1936, one of eight winners of a Fresco Competition.

77. Ezio Buscio. *Giovanni Berta.*
   1936, one of eight winners of a Fresco Competition.

78. Ignazio Zuloaga. *Belmonte.*
   1938, Premio di Duce.

79. Felice Casorati. *Nude in an Armchair.*
   1938, Premio del Comune di Venezia.

80. Guglielmo Aba-Novák. *Yoked Bulls.*
   1940, Premio del Capo del Governo.

81. Artur Kampf. *The People's Offering.*
   1942, Premio del Capo del Governo.

82. Georges Braque. *The Chair.*
   1948, Premio Presidenza Consiglio dei Ministri.

83. Henri Matisse. *Still Life with Magnolias.*
   1950, Premio Presidenza Consiglio dei Ministri.

84. Raoul Dufy. *Studio.*
   1952, Premio Presidenza Consiglio dei Ministri.

85. Marino Marini. *Grande Cavallo.*
   1952, Premio del Comune di Venezia.

86. Max Ernst. *Celebes* (1921).
   1954, Premio Presidenza Consiglio dei Ministri.

87. Jean Arp. *L'Orologio* (painted wood, 1924).
   1954, Premio Presidenza Consiglio dei Ministri.

88. Jacques Villon. *Bridge at Beaugincy* (1944).
   1956, Premio Presidenza Consiglio dei Ministri.

89. Lynn Chadwick. *The Inner Eye* (metal and glass).
   1956, Premio Presidenza Consiglio dei Ministri.

90. Osvaldo Licini. *Amalasunta.*
    1958, Premio Presidenza Consiglio dei Ministri.
91. Mark Tobey. *Capricorn.*
    1958, Premio del Comune di Venezia.
92. Jean Fautrier. *W a Da Da.*
    1960, Premio Presidenza Consiglio dei Ministri.
93. Alberto Giacometti. *Seated Woman* (bronze).
    1962, Premio Presidenza Consiglio dei Ministri.
94. Robert Rauschenberg. *Buffalo II.*
    1964, Premio Presidenza Consiglio dei Ministri.
95. Julio Le Parc. *Potential Circles.*
    1966, Premio Presidenza Consiglio dei Ministri.

Endpapers:
Postcard for XII Biennale, 1920.
Mark Rothko, *Saffron.* Painted 1957 (formerly Collection Carlo Cardazzo). Rothko was exhibited at Biennale, 1958.

BIBLIOGRAPHY

Magazines are not included, as the majority of articles are topical and ephemeral, but footnotes in the text provide some references.

1. Biennale Exhibition Catalogues. Venice, 1895 to date.
2. Alessandro Stella. *Chronistoria della Esposizione Internazionale d'Arte della Città di Venezia 1895-1912*. Venice, n.d. (*ca.* 1912).
3. Arturo Lancellotti. *La Biennale Veneziane dell'Ante Guerra. Dalla I alla XI*. Venice, 1928.
4. Arturo Lancellotti. *La Biennale Veneziane del Dopo Guerra*. Venice, 1926.
5. *La Biennale di Venezia, Storia e Statistiche*. Venice, n.d. (1932).
6. Nino Barbantini. *Biennali*. Venice, 1945.
7. Ivana Mononi. *L'Orientamento del Gusto Moderno Attraverso le Biennali di Venezia*. Thesis, Università degli Studi di Milano. 1956. (Copy in the Archivio Storico d'Arte Contemporanea della Biennale.) The substance was published as *L'Orientamento del Gusto Attraverso le Biennali*. Milan, 1957.
8. André de Ridder. *De Levende Kunst Gezien te Venetie*. 2 vols. Brussels, 1958. (Survey of the 1948-56 Biennales.)
9. Romolo Bazzoni. *60 Anni della Biennale di Venezia*. Venice, 1962. (The indispensable book on Biennale history.)
10. Virgilio Guzzi. *Arte d'oggi, storie di otto Biennali*. Rome, 1964. ("Soliloqui e dibattimenti," 1948-62.)

APPENDIX

some statistics

DATE	NUMBER OF VISITORS	TOTAL WORKS EXHIBITED	TOTAL NUMBER OF SALES	NUMBER OF ITALIAN WORKS EXHIBITED
1895	224,327	516	186	188
1897	265,064	892	239	204
1899	309,141	1134	254	575
1901	289,071	889	428	432
1903	289,553	916	388	533
1905	263,827	1234	704	473
1907	357,356	1295	525	493
1909	457,960	1759	1209	704
1910	345,851	2036	657	771
1912	431,742	2027	869	1047
1914	337,904	2474	612	1074
1920	240,510	1805	682	739
1922	380,544	2564	575	1127
1924	319,853	3307	885	1244
1926	201,025	2573	367	1007
1928	172,841	2725	350	1023
1930	193,003	3000	462	1365
1932	249,960	3229	516	1579
1934	361,917	4222	600	1813
1936	194,702	3604	511	1859
1938	175,619	3388	453	1203
1940	87,391	3182	439	1754
1942	76,679	3560	803	2520
1948	216,471	3065	450	1607
1950	171,414	3342	401	1413
1952	183,107	3439	562	1132
1954	171,600	3638	625	1283
1956	188,487	4564	721	1945
1958	172,545	3240	490	855
1960	150,902	2898	684	736
1962	154,000	3214	685	880
1964	161,772	2918	392	727
1966	181,383	2785	...	914

INDEX

Aba-Novák, Guglielmo, *80*
Abstract Expressionism, 140, 144, 145
  post-, 146–47
Accademia de Belle Arti, 25
Action Française group, 101
Action Painting, 140, 141
Aero Pittori, 108–9, 119 (n.27)
Aeroportraits, simultaneous, 116
Afro, 140
Ahrens, Ellen W., 128
Alloway, Lawrence, 19, 154 (n.6)
Alma-Tadema, Sir Lawrence, 54 (n.9),
  141
American Artists in Paris, theme show
  in 1899, 52
American Magazine of Art, The, 118
  (n.1)
American pavilion, *see* United States
  pavilion
Anderton, Isabella, 54 (n.14)
Angeli, Franco, 147
Anglada-Camarasa, Herman, *54*
Apollinaire, Guillaume, 126
Apollonio, Umbro, 22, 24, 29 (n.16),
  151
Appel, 123
Aranda, J. J., 54 (n.9)
Archipenko, Aleksandr, 95
Architectural Design, 154 (n.6)
Architecture
  of pavilions, 17–18, 49–50
  of other expositions, 34–35
Argentina, 146, 153
Arkus, Leon Anthony, 131 (n.17)
Arnold, Matthew, 122
Arp, Jean, 136, 139, *87*
Art autré, 140, 144
Art Bulletin, 91 (n.4)
Art Dealers Association of America, 21
Art Décoratif, L', 55 (n.21)
Art informel, 140, 144, 151, 152
  post-, 146, 152
Art Nouveau, 47, 48, 49, 50, 87
Arte straniera, 111
Artists' Union, 102, 104
Austin, Darrell, 138

Austrian pavilion, 23, 111, 115, 134,
  142, 146
Austria-Hungary, 51
Ay-o, 151, *41*

Bacon, F., 123, 136
Bakst, Leon, 55 (n.20)
Balestrieri, Lionello, 90, *16*
Balla, 107, 119 (n.27)
Barbantini, Nino, 95, 118 (n.6), 145
Barbieri, Contardo, *74*
Barbisan, Giovanni, 103, *76*
Barbizon School, 41, 42, 52
Baroque revival, 94, 108
Barr, Alfred H., jr., 154 (n.4)
Bartels, Hans von, *59*
Baudelaire, Charles, 37, 38
Bauhaus, 108
Bazzoni, Romolo, 52, 95, 96, 110,
  119 (n.30), 154 (n.1)
Beaux, Cecilia, 112, 128
Beckmann, Max, 135
Behrens, Peter, 50
Belgian pavilion, 52, 53, 111, 112,
  115, 118 (n.3), 136
Benedetta, 119 (n.27)
Benlliure, José, 54 (n.9)
Benson, Frank W., 128
Berenson, Bernard, 97
Bernard, Emile, 95, 99, 143
Bernstamm, L., 54 (n.9)
Besnard, Paul-Albert, 49
Bezzi, Bartolomeo, 32, 33, 54 (n.1),
  94
Bianco, Pieretto, 50
Biase, Giuseppe, *61*
Bienal Americana De Arte, Cordoba,
  153
Bienal de Sao Paulo, 15, 29 (n. 3),
  142
Biennale San Marino, 151
Biennale, Venice:
  1895, 31–35, 43–46
  1897, 43, 48, 51, 52, 94
  1899, 46, 48, 52
  1901, 47, 48, 52

Note: Numerals in italics refer to the illustrations.

Biennale, Venice: (contd)
  1903, 47, 48–49, 52
  1905, 115
  1907, 47, 49–50, 115, 128
  1909, 47, 50
  1910, 47, 51, 53, 99
  1912, 47, 50, 52–53
  1914, 47, 52, 53
  1920, 94, 95, 111
  1922, 94, 95, 111
  1924, 94, 95, 96
  1926, 95, 106, 111
  1930, 93–94, 96, 103–4, 105–6, 110, 111, 112, 113, 114, 128, *32*
  1932, 94, 95, 104–5, 108–9, 111
  1934, 95, 105, 111, 112–13, 114
  1936, 94, 95
  1938, 95, 105, 109–10, 111, 113, 114
  1940, 94, 114, 115, *33*
  1942, 115, 116–17, 133
  1948, 134, 137–39
  1950, 135, 137, 139, 142
  1952, 137, 139, 140, 142
  1954, 122, 136–37, 139
  1956, 136, 137, 140
  1958, 144
  1960, 142, 144–45
  1962, 23–24, 146
  1964, 22, 146–47, 149–50, 152
  1966, 13–14, 18, 20
  1968, 19, 24–28
Bille, Eiler, 138
Birolli, Renato, 140
Blanc, Charles, 91 (n.4)
Blaue Reiter, 135
Boase, T. S. R., 36
Boccioni, Umberto, 106, 107
Böcklin, Arnold, 33
Boimé, Albert, 91 (n.4)
Boldini, Giovanni, 52, 54 (n.9), 94
Bolognese School, 87
Bonnard, Pierre, 95
Bordiga, Giovanni, 33, 95
Bosch, Hieronymus, 136
Bouguereau, Adolphe William, 42
Brangwyn, Sir Frank, 49
Braque, Georges, 134, 137, 148, *82*
Brasillach, Robert, 101
Brazilian pavilion, 18, 142
Bright, David E., 23
Brinkman, A. E., 55 (n.16)
Brinton, Crane, 155 (n.11)
British pavilion, 18, 49, 52, 111, 112, 115, 116, 134, 136, 140, 141, 142
Bucci, Anselmo, 96
Burlington Magazine, The, 131 (n.9)
Burnand, Eugène, *11*
Burne-Jones, Sir Edward, 48, 54 (n.9), 90
Buscio, Ezio, 77

Calder, Alexander, 139
Camerata degli Artisti, 108

Canadian pavilion, 18, 146
Canegrati, Amerigo, 106, *70*
Canogar, Rafael, 142
Carbonaro, R., 18
Carcano, Filippo, 54 (n.9)
Carnegie, Andrew, 127
Carnegie Institute, 112, 131 (n.17)
Carolus-Duran, 33, 40, 42, 52, 54 (n.9)
Carpanetti, Arnaldo, 104, *69*
Carra, Carlo, 97, 98, 116, 134, 139, 154 (n.1), *28*
Carrière, Eugène, 52
Casanova, Achille, 48, *17*
Cascella, Andrea, 152
Cascella, Tommaso, 105, *73*
Casorati, Felice, 154 (n.1), *79*
Cassiers, Henri, 125
Cassirer, Ernst, 88
Castelli, Leo, 20
Castelli Gallery, 21, 149
Castelnuovo, Enrico, 32
Catalogues
  Agency, 141
  Barbizon Revisited, 54 (n.12)
  Muse or Ego, 54 (n.10)
  National Collection of Fine Arts, 15, 23
  Pavilion, 141
  Sao Paulo 9th Bienal, 15
  III Internationalen Kunstausstellung, 33
  U. S. requirements for, 29 (n.3)
  Venice
    1895, 33, 34
    1901, 40
    1930, 96
    1942, 116–17
    1964, 29 (n.3)
Censorship, 32, 46, 105–106
Central Pavilion, 17, 23, 98–99, 119 (n.29)
  1897, 51
  1914, 53
  1928, *26*
  1930, 110, *34*
  1932, 94
  1934, 112
  1935, 111–12
  1940, 115–16
  1950, 140
  1958, 144
  1960, 142
  1964, 147, 150
Cézanne, Paul, 95, 98, 99, 102, 113
Chadwick, Lynn, 140, 142, *89*
Chagall, Marc, 134
Chardin, Jean-Baptiste Siméon, 148
Chavannes, Puvis de, 48
Chicago World's Columbian Exposition, 34–35, 36
Chini, Galileo, 50, *19*
Chirico, Giorgio di, 97, 100, 134, 135–36
Ciano, Count Galeazzo, 116

Ciardi, Guglielmo, 33, 40
Cirilli, Guido, 34, *2*
Claus, Emile, *51*
Clert, Iris, 24
Cobra movement, 138
Cocteau, Jean, 101
Commissione per l'arte figurativa, post-
    World War II, 154 (n.1)
Commission, 1895, 15–16, 32, 54
    (n.1)
Committee of Patronage, 1895, 40
Constable, Rosalind, 23, 24
Constable, W. G., 101
Conti, Primo, *65*
Convegno di Poesia, 16
Cooper, Douglas, 123
Cordoba, Bienal Americana de Arte,
    153
Corneille, Pierre, 101
Corot, Jean, 52
Corpora, Antonio, 140
Cortona, Pietro da, 108
Courbet, Gustave, 27, 44, 53, 136, 153
Crafts in the Biennale, 114
Crane, Walter, 33, 43, *19*
Criticism
    a definition of, 131 (n.16)
    exhibitions as occasions for, 36–39,
        122–23
    modern, 87, 126–27
    variables affecting, 88–89
Crowds, types of, 123
Crystal Palace, 35, 36
Cubism, 47, 102, 135, 137
Cuixart, Modest, 142
Czechoslovakian pavilion, 111

Dali, Salvador, 89
Danish pavilion, 18, 51, 111, 115,
    119 (n.29), 138
D'Annunzio, Gabriele, 45
Daudet, Alphonse, 95
Davie, Alan, 138
Davies, Marion, 113
Davis, Stuart, 112
de la Siseranne, Robert, 45
Dealers' influence on jurors, 20–22
Decoration of pavilions, 48–50
Degas, 86, 95, 98
Delacroix, Eugène, 37
Dell'Acqua, Cesare, 54 (n.9)
Dell'Armi, Giovanni Battista, 134
Delvaux, Paul, 112
Denis, Maurice, 95, 99–100, 101
Denmark, *see* Danish pavilion
Depero, Fortunato, 94, 107, 119
    (n.27)
Derain, André, 100
Despiau, Charles, 95
di Chirico, Giorgio, 97, 100, 134,
    135–36
Diaghilev, Serge, 55 (n.20)
Diderot, Denis, 39
Domus, 155 (n.10)
Donahue, Kenneth, 19

Dongen, Kees Van, 95
Dottori, Gherardo, 104, 119 (n.27),
    71
Dova, Gianni, 140
Dubois, Paul, 54 (n.9)
Dubuffet, Jean, 139, 143
Duce, Il, *see* Mussolini
Duchamp, Marcel, 125
Dudreville, Leonardo, 96
Dufy, Raoul, 137, *84*
Dutch pavilion, 51, 112, 115, 118 (n.3)
Dzamonja, 142

Eakins, Thomas, 129
Ecole des Beaux-Arts, 86, 87
Economist, The, 29 (n.1)
Egger-Lienz, Albin, *63*
Egyptian pavilion, 17, 140
Eliot, T. S., 122
Emmerich, André, Gallery, 21
England, *see* British pavilion
Ensor, James, 53
Epstein, Jacob, 112
Ernst, Max, 136, 137, *86*
Eschenburg, Theodor, 94
Esposizione Biennale Internazionale
    d'Arte, 113
Esposizione Internazionale d'Arte
    Decorativa Moderna, Turin, 50
Esposizione Internazionale di Bella
    Arte, Rome, 47
Estève, Maurice, 137
Exposition Universelle, Paris, 36–37,
    41
Expressionism, 94
    Flemish, 135
    German, 47

Fabbri, Algenore, 140
Fahlström, Oyvind, 151
Far, Isabelle, 136
Fascism and the Biennale, 93–117
Fascist Futurism, 106–10
Fassbender, Joseph, 152
Fautrier, Jean, 144–45, *92*
Fauvism, Les Fauves, 129, 135
Favretto, Giacomo, 33, 40, 52, 90,
    145, *12, 13*
Feito, Luis, 142
Ferenczy, Károly, 115, *55*
Festa, Tano, 147
Fillia, 109, 119 (n.27)
Film Festival, 16, 114
Fine art vs. popular culture, 121–30
Fine-ottocento, 50
Fiocco, Giuseppe, 154 (n.1)
First Futurist Exhibition of Plastic Art
    of the War, 1916, 110
Florian, Café, 21, 31, 40
Fogazzaro, Antonio, 46
Fontana, Lucio, 119 (n.24), 140, 143,
    144, 148, 151, *39*
Forain, Jean-Louis, 95
Force, Mrs. Juliana, 113
Formes, 55 (n.16), 100–1

Forty Years of the Biennale, 1935, 111–12
Fould, Achille, 41
Fradeletto, Antonio, 16, 32, 33, 49–50, 52, 54 (n.1)
Fragiacomo, Pietro, 33, 40, 49, 54 (n.1), 90, 94, *24*
France, *see* French pavilion
Francesca, Piero della, 102
Franco, General, 114
Frankenthaler, 21
French pavilion, 18, 49, 53, 95, 111, 115, 116, 134, 136, 137
French Salon, 35 (*see also* Salon art)
French School, 100
Fronte Nuovo dell'Arte, 137–38
Fry, Roger, 102, 119 (n.20)
Funi, Achille, 96, 116
Futurism, Futurists, 93, 94, 97, 99, 106–10, 112, 125–26, 135, *34*

Galerie Lawrence, 21
Galleria d'Arte Moderna, Venice, 46, 145
Galleries
 Castelli, Leo, 21
 Emmerich, André, 21
 Grand Central, 119 (n.29)
 Janis, Sidney, 145
 Lawrence, 21
 Parsons, Betty, 14, 154 (n.5)
 René, Denise, 14
 Sonnabend, Ileana, 21
 Svensky-Franska, 15
Gallery of Modern Portraits, 52
Gans, Herbert J., 84
Gauguin, Paul, 95, 100, 101
Gazzettino, Il, 119 (n.32)
Geldzahler, Henry, 22, 122
Georges, Waldemar, 100
Gerard, Helen, 118 (n.1)
German pavilion, 17, 52, 53, 111, 115, 118 (n.3), 134, 136
Gérôme, Jean-Léon, 89, 141
Geske, 19
Giacometti, Alberto, 139, 146, *93*
Giacometti, Augusto, 112
Giarrizzo, Manlio, 105, *75*
Gioli, F., *16*
Giotto, 97
Giovanelli, Alberto, 145
Gischia, Leon, 137
Giustiniani, V., *16*
Gladstone, William, 36
Glasgow School, 50
Glueck, Grace, 29 (n.6, 7, 8, 9)
Goebbels, Joseph, 117
Goldberg, Betsey, 54 (n.3)
Goncourt, Edmond and Jules de, 95
Gorky, Arshile, 138, 139, 146
Gossip and the Biennale, 20–22
Government Agency for the Biennale, 15–16, 22, 31–32, 113
Goya, Francisco, 143
Grand Central Galleries, 119 (n.29)

Graziani, Alfio Paolo, 104, *72*
Great Exhibition, London, 36–37, 38
Greek pavilion, 17, 111, 112
Greenberg, Clement, 122, 149, 150
Greene, Graham, 147
Grimani, Filippo, 52
Gris, Juan, 102
Grosso, Giacomo, 46, 89, *9*
Grosvenor, Thomas, 51
Gruppo N, 147, 151
Gruppo T, 147, 151
Guerrisi, Michele, *68*
Guggenheim, Michelangelo, 54 (n.1)
Guggenheim, Peggy, 138
Guggenheim International Award, 22
Guggenheim Museum, 18, 19
Guston, Philip, 145
Guttuso, Renato, 136–37, 140, 147, *38*

Haas, J. H. L. de, 54 (n.9)
Haftmann, Werner, 47
Hahn, Otto, 20
Haller, Herman, 111
Hals, Franz, 42
Harper's Magazine, 155 (n.9)
Harper's Monthly, 54 (n.3)
Hauser, Arnold, 91 (n.5)
Hazlitt, William, 121, 122
Hearst, William Randolph, 113
Hemingway, Ernest, 114
Henner, J. J., 54 (n.9)
Henry, George, 51
Herbert, Robert L., 54 (n.12)
Herkomer, Hubert von, 33, 52
Historical Archives of Contemporary Art, 22
Hitler, 7
Hodler, Ferdinand, 48
Hoflehner, Rudolf, 142
Hofmann, Hans, 145
Hogarth, William, 85
Holland, *see* Dutch pavilion
Homer, Winslow, 128
Honour, Hugh, 55 (n.20)
Hopper, Edward, 112
Hopps, Walter, 29 (n.3)
Horta, Victor, 50
Hubacher, Hermann, 111
Hundertwasser, 23, 24, 146
Hungarian pavilion, 17, 52, 111, 114, 115
Hunt, William Holman, 41

Il Duce, *see* Mussolini
Impressionism, 85, 86, 97, 98, 125–26
 French, 44, 47, 53, 134
 German, 44
 Italian, 44
Ingres, J. A. D., 37, 90
Instituto Torcuato Di Tella, Buenos Aires, 153
Internationalen Kunstausstellung, Der III, 33

Israels, Jozef, 42, 45, 54 (n.9), 57
Italianità, l', 95, 97, 112

Jacobsen, Egill, 138
Janis, Sidney, Gallery, 145
Japanese pavilion, 18, 51, 146
Jewish Museum, 149
Johns, Jasper, 149, 151
Jorn, Asger, 22
Jurors, influence on, 21–22

Kahnweiler, Daniel-Henry, 102
Kampf, Artur, 115, 81
Kandinsky, Wassily, 83
Karl Theodorus, 33
Karolis, Adolfo de, 60
Kemeny, Zoltan, 152
Kennedy, John F., 151
Kent, Rockwell, 112
Khnopff, Fernand, 48, 90, 125, 131
   (n.15)
Kienholz, Edward, 19
Klee, Paul, 112, 134, 136, 146
Klein, Yves, 15
Klimt, Gustav, 48, 53, 99, 146, 21
Kline, Franz, 144, 145
Kokoschka, Oskar, 134
Kooning, Willem de, 122, 123, 139
Kramer, Hilton, 20
Kröyer, Peter Severin, 40, 54 (n.9),
   20

Lancellotti, Arturo, 95
Lange, Julius, 45
Laszlo, Philip de, 115, 56
La Touche, Gaston, 44, 129, 130, 52
Laurenti, Cesare, 45, 54 (n.1)
Lausanne, Salon International de
   Galeries-pilotes, 14–15
Lavery, Sir John, 52, 128
La Voce, 106
Lawrence, Galerie, 21
Leempoels, Jef, 48, 90, 14
Léger, Fernand, 102
Leibl, Wilhelm, 52
Leighton, Lord, 40, 43, 54 (n.9)
Lenbach, Franz von, 52, 53
Leonardi, Leoncillo, 154 (n.1)
Leonardo da Vinci, 96
Le Parc, Julio, 20, 151, 95
Levi, Marco, 54 (n.1)
Lichtenstein, Roy, 20, 151, 40
Licini, Osvaldo, 90
Liebermann, Max, 33, 45, 54 (n.9),
   111, 64
Life, 84, 91 (n.1)
Life International, 29 (n.12)
Longhi, Roberto, 102, 134, 154 (n.1)
L'Ora, 29 (n.22)
Lorca, Federico Garcia, 114
Los Angeles County Museum, 19
Louis, Morris, 21, 149, 150
Louvre, Grande Galerie, 38
Lowry, Bates, 41
Ludwig I, King, 33

Maccari, Cesare, 54 (n.9)
Macdonald, Frances E., 48
Macdonald, Margaret, 48
Mackintosh, Charles Rennie, 48, 50
Magritte, René, 112, 136
Malerba, Gian Emilio, 96
Malevich, Kasimir, 83, 108
Malraux, André, 42, 144
Mamoulian, Rouben, 114
Manessier, Alfred, 137, 141, 146
Manet, Edouard, 42, 86, 95
Manzù, Giacomo, 139, 154 (n.1)
Maraini, Antonio, 16, 96, 110, 116,
   117
Maremont, Arnold A., 23
Margherita, Queen of Italy, 31, 5
Maria, Marius de, 32, 34, 54 (n.1),
   94, 1
Marin, John, 140
Marinetti, F. T., 106–10 passim, 115,
   119 (n.27), 126, 8
Marini, Marino, 139, 154 (n.1), 85
Marsili, Emilio, 32, 33, 54 (n.1), 44
Marussig, Pietro, 96
Masaccio, 97, 98
Mathéy, François, 20
Matisse, Henri, 95, 98, 128, 137, 83
Maurer, Alfred H., 128
Max Joseph I, 33
Mazzanti, R., 16
McEvoy, Arthur Ambrose, 94
McNair, J. Herbert, 50
Mesdag, H. W., 54 (n.9)
Messer, Thomas M., 19
Metaphysical painting, 97, 134, 135
Mexican murals, 102
Michelangelo, 147
Michetti, Francesco Paolo, 40, 45, 52,
   54 (n.9), 94, 42
Milesi, Alessandro, 45, 90, 25, 43
Millais, Sir John Everett, 41, 54 (n.9)
Millares, Manuel, 142
Minguzzi, Luciano, 140
Minio, Giuseppe, 32, 54 (n.1)
Miró, Joan, 136, 139
Misoneists, 107, 119 (n.23)
Modigliani, Amedeo, 95, 98, 106
Moillet, Louis, 146
Mondrian, Piet, 83, 112
Monet, Claude, 42, 45, 95, 126
Mononi, Ivana, 55 (n.18)
Monteverde, Giulio, 54 (n.9)
Monticelli, Adolphe Joseph Thomas,
   53
Moore, Henry, 112, 134, 138
Morandi, Giorgio, 134, 154 (n.1)
Moreau, Gustave, 48, 54 (n.9)
Morelli, Domenico, 42, 45, 54 (n.9)
Morlotti, Ennio, 140
Mortensen, Richard, 138
Mostra Internazionale d'Arte Cinema-
   tografica, 16
Munch, Edvard, 123
Munich Glaspalast, 33
Munkacsy, Michael, 40, 54 (n.9)

Munthe, Richard, 45
Musée Cantonal des Beaux-Arts, Lausanne, 14
Musée des Copies, 91 (n.4)
Museum of Modern Art, New York, 136, 149, 154 (n.4)
Music Festival, 16, 114
Mussolini, Arnaldo, 116
Mussolini, Benito, 16, 96–97, 103–10 *passim,* 114, 116, 6
Mussolini, Vittorio, 110

Napoleon, 38
Nash, Paul, 116
National Collection of Fine Arts, 15, 18, 19, 23
National pavilions, *see* individual countries
Nazism and art, 102
Neo-Impressionism, 53, 125–26
New Realism, 147
New York Sun, The, 126
New York Times, The, 19, 29 (n.7)
Newsweek, 24
Noland, Kenneth, 21, 149, 150
Nolde, Emil, 118 (n.3), 139
Nomellini, Plinio, *19*
Nono, Luigi, 33, *50*
Norway, 51
Novecento Italiano group, 96
Nudes in the Biennale, 105–6
Ny-Carlsberg Foundation, 119 (n.29)

Olitski, Jules, 21
One-man shows, 51–52
Op Art, 85
Ora, L', 29 (n.22)
Orozco, José Clemente, 102
Orsi, Pietro, 96, 110
Ortega y Gasset, *42,* 84

Palazzo dell'Esposizione, 35, 38, 52
Palazzo Pesaro, 145
Palluchini, Rodolfo, 55 (n.23), 133, 138, 154 (n.1)
Papadopoli, Nicolo, 54 (n.1)
Parc, Julio Le, 20, 151, *95*
Parsons, Betty, 154 (n.5)
Parsons, Betty, Gallery, 14
Pasini, Alberto, 54 (n.9)
Passini, Ludwig, 54 (n.9)
Pater, Walter, 87
Paulsen, Julius, 45
Pavilions
  as architecture, 17–18, 49–51
  national, *see* particular country
Paxton, Sir Joseph, 35
Pedersen, Carl-Henning, 138
Permeke, Constant, 118 (n.3)
Peterssen, Eilif, 54 (n.9)
Pevsner, Nikolaus, 29 (n.2)
Pezzo, Lucio del, 147, 151
Philpot, Glyn, 112
Pica, Vittorio, 95

Picasso, Pablo, 98, 106, 114, 128, 134, 154 (n.4)
Pietzsch, Richard, 111
Pignon, Edouard, 137
Pinder, Wilhelm, 88
Pissarro, Camille, 86, 87
Pistoletto, 151
Pitt, William, 151
Pittsburgh International, 112, 127–29, 142
Pittura Metafisica group, 97
Pius X, 32
Plato, 131 (n.14)
Plein-air landscape, 44
Polish pavilion, 111, 115
Pollock, Jackson, 138, 139, 141, 148
Pomodoro, Arnaldo, 152
Ponge, Francis, 144
Ponti, Giovanni, 133, 154 (n.1)
Pop Art, 26, 85, 91 (n.1), 147, 150
Porter, Charlotte, 55 (n.17)
Post-Impressionism, 93, 95, 98, 101, 106, 134
Poussin, Nicolas, 102
Poussinistes, 121
Prampolini, Enrico, 94, 107–10 *passim,* 116, 119 (n.27), *31, 36*
Pranishnikoff, Ivan P., 54 (n.9)
Praz, Mario, 40, 43
Pre-Raphaelite Brotherhood, 41
Prizes, special, 103–4
  given by collectors, 23
  maternity, 103, 106
  Fascist Party, 104, 105
Programma
  1930, 96, 100, 117
  1942, 117
Puvis de Chavannes, 48

Raffaeli, Jean François, 128
Ragghianti, Carlo Ludovico, 154 (n.1)
Raphael, 50
Rauschenberg, Robert, 20, 91 (n.1), 148–52 *passim, 155* (n.9), *94*
Raysse, Martial, 151
Recalcati, Antonio, 147
Reid, Norman, 20
Rembrandt, 87
René, Denise, Gallery, 14
Renoir, 53, 95, 98, 113
Repin, Ilya Efimovich, 43
Restany, Pierre, 150, 151, 155 (n.10)
Rey, Robert, 101
Reynolds, Sir Joshua, 42, 123
Riopelle, Jean-Paul, 146
Rivera, Diego, 102
Rodin, 48, 52
Romagnoli, Giuseppe, 48, *17*
Romanticism, Italian, 43
Rosenberg, Harold, 15, 124
Rosenquist, James, 147
Rossetti, William Michael, 45
Rosso, Medardo, 53, 135
Roszak, Theodore, 142
Rotella, Mimmo, 147

Rothenstein, Sir William, 112
Rothko, Mark, 138, 144
Rotta, Silvio, 45
Rouault, Georges, 134
Roumanian pavilion, 17, 111, 115
Rousseau, le douanier, 135
Rousseau, Théodore, 41
Royal Academy, The, London, 35, 100
Royal decrees concerning the Biennale,
     113–14
Rubbiani, A., *17*
Rubenistes, 121
Rudé, George, 123
Ruskin, John, 36
Russian pavilion, 17, 51, 53, 111, 115
Russolo, 107
Rysselberghe, Theo van, 53

Sala del Nord, 51
Salon art, 35, 42–43, 48, 49, 50, 53,
     83, 86, 88–89, 93, 95, 98, 113,
     125, 129, 141
Salon International de Galeries-pilotes,
     14
San Marino Biennale, 151
Santomaso, Giuseppe, 138
Sao Paulo Bienal, 15, 29 (n.3), 142
Sargent, J. S., 42, 52, *58*
Sartorio, Giulio Aristide, 44, 49, 89,
     46
Sartre, Jean-Paul, 146
Saura, Antonio, 142
Savelli, Angelo, 152
Savinio, Alberto, 97
Schapiro, Meyer, 89, 91 (n.7)
Schiele, Egon, 134, 146
Schönleber, Gustav, 54 (n.9)
School of Laethem St. Martin, 118
     (n.3)
School of Paris, 100, 128, 135, 140
Schrotter, Riccardo, 98, *29*
Scialoja, Toti, 140
Sciltian, Gregorio, 116
Scotland, 51
Scott, David, 19
Scull, Robert C., 23
Segantini, Giovanni, 45
Segonzac, Dunoyer de, 111
Sei Pittori del'900 (1924), 96
Seibezzi, Fioravante, 67
Seitz, William, 29 (n.3)
Selvatico, Luigi, 47
Selvatico, Riccardo, 16, 32, 46, 52
Semeghini, Pio, 154 (n.1)
Seurat, Georges, 86, 87, 91 (n.4), 126
Severini, Gino, 106
Sézanne, Augusto, 32, 33, 48, 54
     (n.1), *17*
Shahn, Ben, 122
Sickert, W. R., 112
Sidney Janis Gallery, 145
Signac, Paul, 86
Signorini, Telemaco, *49*
Sindicati delle Belle Arti, 102

Siqueiros, David, 102
Sironi, Mario, 96
Siseranne, Robert de la, 45
Skeaping, John, 112
Sluytens, Jan, 111
Smet, Gustave de, 118 (n.3)
Smithsonian Institution, 18
Socrates, 124
Soffici, Ardengo, 106
Solomon, Alan, 29 (n.3), 149, 150
Somenzi, 119 (n.27)
Sonnabend, Ileana, Gallery, 21
Sorolla, Joaquin, 40
Soviet pavilion, *see* Russian pavilion
Soyer, Raphael, 138
Spadini, Armando, *66*
Spanish pavilion, 18, 51, 111, 115,
     141, 142–43
Sport Fascista, 104
Stanton, Blair Hughes, 111
Statistics, 193
Stedelijk Museum, Amsterdam, 20
Stella, Alessandro, 40, 118 (n.4)
Stella, Frank, 91 (n.1)
Stevenson, Harold, 24
Stucky, Giovanni, 54 (n.1)
Student disturbance, 1968, 24–28
Student manifesto, 1968, 25
Studio, 54 (n.14)
Suprematist art, 108
Surrealism, 112, 136
Svensky-Franska Gallery, 15
Swedish pavilion, 51, 52, 111, 115
Swiss pavilion, 18, 112, 115, 134, 142
Symbolism, 47, 48, 90

Tachisme, 140, 141
Tack, Augustus Vincent, 112
Tamburlini, A., *18*
Tàpies, Antonio, 142, 143
Tarbell, Edmund C., 128
Tate Gallery, The, 20
Tato, S. G., 109, 119 (n.27), *35*
Tharrats. J. J., 142
Theater Festival, 114
Tiepolo, G. B., 108
Time, 24, 91 (n.1)
Tito, Ettore, 33, 40, 44, 45, 94, 116,
     22, 23
Tobey, Mark, 138, *91*
Tomkins, Calvin, 155 (n.9)
Torres, Giulio, *3*
Tosi, Arturo, 116, *27*
Toulouse-Lautrec, Henri de, 95
Trentacoste, Domenico, 45, *16, 48*
Tuchman, Maurice, 19

Uhde, Fritz von, 54 (n.9)
Umberto I, King of Italy, 31, 50, *5*
Ungaretti, Giuseppe, 16
United Arab Republic pavilion, 17,
     140
United States Information Agency, 149

United States pavilion, 18, 22, 26, 27, 111, 112, 115, 116, 119 (n.29), 138, 141, 142, 144, 149–50

Valori Plastici group, 97
van de Woestyne, Gustave, 118 (n.3)
van den Berghe, Frits, 118 (n.3)
van der Stappen, Charles, 54 (n.9)
Van Dongen, Kees, 95
Van Gogh, Vincent, 42, 100, 118 (n.3), 123, 129–30, 143
van Haanen, C. C., 54 (n.9)
van Rysselberghe, Theo, 53
Vantongerloo, Georges, 139
Variables affecting one's relationship to art, 88–89
Vedova, Emilio, 138, 140
Velasquez, Diego, 42, 148
Venice Art and Company, 46
Venturi, Adolfo, 45
Venturi, Lionello, 154 (n.1)
Veth, Jan, 54 (n.13)
Villegas, José, 54 (n.9)
Villon, Jacques, 137, 88
Virgili, Giuseppe, 105, 37
Vittorio Emanuele III, King of Italy, 16, 50, 113, 145, 8
Voce, La, 106
Volpi di Misurata, Giuseppe, 16

War Artists' Commission in England, 116
Wellek, René, 119 (n.21)
Werner, Anton von, 54 (n.9)
Whistler, James McNeill, 45, 48, 52, 89, 10
Whitney Museum, 113
Wildt, Adolfo, 110, 30
Winckelmann, Johann, 37, 38
Wind, Edgar, 124
Woestyne, Gustave van de, 118 (n.3)
Wols, 15, 144
Wood, Francis Derwent, 51
Working Committee, 1895, 33, 34
World War I, 40, 42, 47, 52, 101, 126
World War II, 22, 42, 88, 93, 101, 107, 115–16, 133–34, 139
W. P. A. Federal Arts Project, 102

Yugoslavian pavilion, 17, 111, 115, 142

Zadkine, Ossip, 95, 139
Zandomeneghi, Federico, 53
Zanetti, Giuseppe, 62
Zervos, Christian, 154 (n.4)
Zezzos, Alessandro, 33
Zola, Emile, 95
Zorn, Anders, 40, 52, 54 (n.9), 45
Zotto, Antonio Dal, 33, 54 (n.1)
Zuloaga, Ignacio, 111, 114, 78